Turning Point

Turning Point

Essays on a New Unitarian Universalism

Fredric Muir, Editor

Skinner House Books
Boston

www.skinnerhouse.org

Printed in the United States

Cover design by Kathryn Sky-Peck
Text design by Suzanne Morgan

print ISBN: 978-1-55896-766-3
eBook ISBN: 978-1-55896-767-0

6 5 4 3
18 17 16

Library of Congress Cataloging-in-Publication Data

Names: Muir, Fredric John, editor.
Title: Turning point : essays on a new Unitarian Universalism / edited by
    Fredric Muir.
Description: Boston : Skinner House Books, 2016. | Includes bibliographical
    references.
Identifiers: LCCN 2015017620| ISBN 9781558967663 (pbk. : alk. paper) | ISBN
    9781558967670 (ebook)
Subjects: LCSH: Unitarian Universalist churches.
Classification: LCC BX9842 .T87 2016 | DDC 289.1/32—dc23 LC record avail-
able at http://lccn.loc.gov/2015017620

To Don and Ann Wheat, who set a course and watched me sail,

To Karen, Kristina, Andrew, Pablo, Adele, Oscar, and Rex—my family—who have walked with and sustained me,

To the Unitarian Universalist Church of Annapolis, which is living the challenges of ministry at a turning point,

And to my colleagues in ministry. All royalties from the sale of this book benefit the Sustaining the Call endowment of the Unitarian Universalist Ministers Association.

—FM

CONTENTS

Foreword

How did we come to be who we are? One way to think about our identity is that we are storied selves. Our identities are formed by stories received from our culture via our families, our peers, and our history. These stories about race, gender, religion, generational differences, sexual orientation, ethnicity, and class work consciously and unconsciously to form us.

We can think of becoming human in this way: Multiple, complex, and sometimes competing stories form both our individual identity and our group identity. They also teach us values and meaning. These stories come from our families of origin, our peers on the playground, our mentors and teachers and guides. They come from the culture in which we live, from television and social media, from history and myth. They are stories about gender, birth order, race/ethnicity; stories about our history and shared quests, and about what our family system values; stories about failure and recovery, about discovery and destiny, about faith and ethics. These different narratives overlap and critique each other, making us ultimately who we are.

As we grow and develop, we test these stories for veracity, we redact and edit these stories in memory and dream, and we reject some of the stories because they no longer "fit." In fact, we are in search of a story that fits, that clarifies our purpose, our vision, our reason to exist. Identity development, then, is the process of testing stories to find our own narrative voice in the speech of and in dialog with others.

In the testing, in the dialog, in the search for fit, our identities shift and are re-storied. For example, the story of faith might say that a good Baptist knows that women don't speak in church, but then a mentor and guide sees my gifts and tells me I must go into the ministry. Affirmation from professors and the profession re-story the "no" into a lived "yes."

The shaping of the individual through stories is only part of the identity development project. There is a communal aspect as well. We share formative narratives in family, in neighborhood, in city, state, and nation. Our national narrative has been shaped by the stories of many peoples: some born here, some who were forced here, some who chose to come here in search of land and a place to thrive. Most of America's peoples, it might be said, yearn for the story that has been called the American Dream. That story promises equality to a broad diversity of races and ethnicities, and accommodates differences in physical and mental ability, gender and sexual orientations, religions and beliefs. That story promises the right to life, liberty, and the pursuit of happiness. That story promises freedom to live, work, learn, play, and grow where one chooses. That story promises that each of us can worship the God of our choice, in the way that we choose, or to choose not to believe in God at all. That story heralds the individual and her inherent worth and dignity. Ralph Waldo Emerson's story and articulation of a theology and philosophy of individualism helped to form the Unitarian Universalist narrative. In an increasingly diverse nation, in which shifting demographics, economic realities, and concerns on the global stage require more and more interdependence, we need to re-story what it means to be an individual in community, what it means to be Unitarian Universalist in these times.

Individualism run amuck has created tensions in the narrative, turned the American dream into a long night of troubled sleep. In short, the experiment that is cultural diversity in American life is riddled with difficulties. Whether one thinks of America as a melting pot, a salad, a mosaic, or a stew, many communities are still quite racially and economically segregated. Discrimination rears its ugly head in the form of hiring practices and hate-crimes. Tolerance for the faith practices of others is sometimes strained at best, and when pushed too far, intolerance erupts in defaced synagogues and burned-down churches.

Our country's increasing diversity adds more complexity to the story of how we will live together in the future. As religious scholar Diana Eck points out in *A New Religious America*, the percentage of foreign-born Americans today is greater than ever before, including during the peak of immigration a century ago. By most United States census projections, visible racial/ethnic minority groups will surpass the population of whites in America somewhere between 2030 and 2050, due to immigration patterns and differential birthrates. In the last decade of the twentieth century, the Hispanic population grew 38.8 percent and has surpassed the African-American population. During the same time period, the Asian population grew 43 percent. In terms of religious diversity, research from Eck's Pluralism Project reveals that in America today, there are about 6 million Muslim Americans, equal to the number of Jews, and greater than the number of either Episcopalians or Presbyterians. The browning of America, the shrinking of the distance between America and the rest of the world, and ever increasing tensions between Muslim and Christian worldviews strain race, ethnic, and faith-group relations in our country. In addition, we see tensions caused by age differences and the clash between those who grew up religiously and those who did not. These strained relations affect all of our identity stories. They invite us to examine our histories, to examine our narrative, to check for "fit." We are invited, all of us, in these days and times, to re-story our identities in order to thrive and survive.

These essays collected by Fredric Muir place Unitarian Universalism in the context of any good story: A beginning, middle, and an end or a telos. If the splendid individualism of Emerson is the beginning, and the end is the Beloved Community, what needs

to happen in order to achieve that end? Muir and his fellow essayists call for a renewed and renewing story about how people know
Unitarian Universalism. He says the language of covenant—which
claims, "As free congregations we promise to one another our
mutual trust and support"—represents the re-storied way forward.

Stories shape and transform our identity, as individuals and as
a community. The stories in this book: Stories of Us—that is, the
stories we tell about ourselves that have brought us to this moment;
Stories of Urgency—the stories that are happening right now; and
Stories of Vision—the stories we tell about what we could be and
that can take us where we want to go—all create a narrative bridge
toward the lofty identity of Beloved Community. They inspire
examination of a group identity in process. Or, perhaps, they call
for the discovery of something already in the DNA of Unitarian
Universalism, something to be extroverted and claimed as "who
we are" for generations to come.

Rev. Dr. Jacqueline J. Lewis
Senior Minister, Middle Collegiate Church, New York City

Introduction

This collection of essays is about the future of Unitarian Universalism, a future to be constructed with the promises shaped by our theology and history, the promises of generosity, pluralism, and imagination. These promises—as promises often are—are a future waiting to be lived and loved. To arrive at this future, we must collectively liberate ourselves from a past that, while bright and bold for some, no longer serves Unitarian Universalism's dream of being a vibrant, twenty-first-century faith. In fact, this past is replete with errors shaped by individualism, exceptionalism, and an aversion to authority. These errors have become barriers preventing us from embracing our future.

I believe that these promises and errors both come from a single source—Ralph Waldo Emerson. His words were bold and fierce, and shaped his generation and now ours. Like biblical scripture, his words have influenced many—indeed, they have shaped a nation. Also like sacred scripture, what we have done to and with the words of "Saint" Emerson, are, perhaps, unintended—the results of his powerful ideas and words. Several generations have taken his ideas and meaning, and interpreted and applied them to their context. This is what we do with words that move and inspire us. And there are consequences to this application.

It might strike you as odd, even inappropriate, to call him *Saint* Emerson—he would certainly protest. While I do this in good fun, my designation has a point: If Unitarian Universalism had a pantheon of those we claim as holy and virtuous—people who showed us another way to live the promise of human life, who saved us from a national and spiritual conspicuous conformity—Emerson would likely top the list. Recognized by many as our nation's first and greatest essayist, his contributions to the development of American and Unitarian Universalist identities are immeasurable. Saint Emerson suggested—often it feels as though he demanded—that we know and name our uniqueness as humans and as Americans and take joy in both. He is both the source of our errors from the past and the inspiration of our promises for the future. It is because of Emerson that this book of essays exists.

Two broad and central supporting themes shaped much—even most—of what Emerson wrote in his letters, journals, sermons, and lectures. First, that the United States must stop living in the shadow of Europe and embrace its own cultural identity. Second, that those who seek spiritual truth and freedom must shed orthodox Christianity. For individuals and for the collective, his messages reinforced the same idea—trust yourself. Every person has all they need to know, so just listen to and believe in yourself. "Your own reason is the voice of God himself," he preached in an 1832 sermon. "[It] speaks to you and to all mankind without an interpreter."

This book explicitly examines the way Unitarian Universalists have responded to the Emersonian philosophy that celebrates and sings the joys and promises of uniqueness and individuality. It implicitly suggests that many of the challenges we struggle with and must address as a people of faith are also challenges that face our nation. In this way—not surprisingly, given Emerson's role as a prophetic voice for liberal religion and US democracy—the histories and future of both our nation and our faith feel intertwined. As a nation and as people of faith, we don't need to follow the ways of others; we are unique. As individuals and as a people, we have all the knowledge and resources we need to shape a meaningful and sustaining identity. As Unitarian Universalists, this Emersonian individualism is embodied in our First Principle, which proclaims the "inherent worth and dignity of every person." As citizens of the United States, individualism—as articulated by Emerson two generations after US independence—is embedded in our foundational documents.

Because Emerson was a patriot and a Unitarian Universalist, because his lectures and books were wildly popular and widespread, because he was claimed by a nation and a religious tradition that embraced the rise of the secular religion called democracy, the lines separating Emerson the American and Emerson the Unitarian Universalist are blurred. And for good reasons: the distinctions are not always clear. The philosophy, theology, and spirituality of Emersonian individualism—that is, the uniqueness and joy of individual differences called individuality—became an ideology, a creed, and a dogma both in the United States and in Unitarian Universalism and is now corrupting both with a short-sighted and shallow vision.

As our nation expanded and as Unitarian Universalism grew, the ideology of individualism—and not the philosophy and theology of individuality—became an accepted and embedded way of believing and living. It became an American way of life and a UU way of believing; it went from the valuing and celebration of differences to the dogma and demands of individual rights. Consequently, the corruption of Emersonian individualism has left us with a twisted definition of what it means to be an American and what it means to be a Unitarian Universalist. This corruption has permeated and shaped our ways of economics, learning, leisure, and religion, which is to say that the perversion of Emersonian individualism is nearly complete and has damaged the promise of our relationships to each other in significant and lasting ways.

This problem is far deeper than a simple lack of communitarian spirit or an overemphasis on rights; this is not just a matter of figuring out a way to balance individual and community needs. Individualism as an ideology, theology, and dogma has been centuries in the making and found expression in Emerson (and transcendentalism) and in the citizens of the United States. The place and time was perfect, and it soared for a long time. Historians and theologians have chronicled the physical and spiritual geography of individualism; for our new nation and its North Atlantic–Anglo peoples, it was an ideology and theology that worked. Some of those who were Unitarian Universalists—or those we claimed as such—eloquently contributed to and supported Emerson's vision.

Yet this individualism has a shadow side, a corrupted practice and articulation of what Emerson said. This twisted understanding of individualism found expression in exceptionalism and an aversion to authority. These expressions have slowed the soaring and have become a danger for both the United States and Unitarian Universalism as each teeters on the brink of free fall. The essays in this book give depth to the errors of individualism and speak to the emerging promises of generosity, pluralism, and imagination as a redeemed individualism. The book concludes with examples of how some Unitarian Universalist communities are living the promises of a restoried Emersonian individualism, a story built on the joy and celebration of individuality.

Three sections—the errors, promises, and future vision of Unitarian Universalism—make up a structure inspired by Marshall Ganz and Jacqueline Lewis. Ganz is a field organizer and a senior lecturer in public policy at the Kennedy School of Government at Harvard University. Lewis is senior minister for vision, worship, and the arts at Middle Collegiate Church in New York City. They both believe in the transforming and organizing power and support found in storytelling—for us, telling the story of Unitarian Universalism. I've adapted Ganz's framework as a way to structure this collection: "Stories of Us," the *Trinity of Errors* that have brought us to this moment; "Stories of Urgency," the *Trinity of Promises* that will take us where we want to go; and "Stories of Vision," *Living the Promises*, the stories happening right now that present breakthrough moments of the Beloved Community, which is to say that they are examples of living the vision we seek. And I owe inspiration from Lewis for her idea of restorying as an effective and deepening way of presenting, embodying, owning, and sustaining our faith.

This book is intended for all who love and care for Unitarian Universalism. The words and examples in these essays may prod and provoke you, they may affirm and support you. I hope they will refresh, inspire, and deepen you. Each essay was composed in a spirit of goodwill and hope, each was written by a person who cares very much about our nation and about Unitarian Universalism. You may have chosen a different way of presentation, different words and expressions; you may react strongly or experience confusion. But, like you, each of the contributors embraces and loves our liberal tradition of faith. *Liberal* is a word that some of us are unlikely, unwilling, or reluctant to use—we rarely hear it anymore as a way of describing our faith. This may be because we have lost an understanding and appreciation for what it means. *Liberal* means open, accepting, broad minded, generous. The Unitarian Universalist way of faith has always been shaped by these qualities, which has been both the joy and the challenge of claiming this faith. These essays reflect this spirit, a spirit that I believe will save Unitarian Universalism for new generations. It's as though these essayists had been sitting in that Harvard Divinity School classroom on Sunday evening, July 15, 1838. They were moved, as were the graduates, by Emerson's message, his pastoral plea to them as the future religious leaders of our still-new nation and our newly organized way of faith. Trust yourselves, he told them; be bold, find a new way that is your way, don't hold back. The students, now graduates soon to be ministers, must have returned to their homes with their heads spinning, excited by Emerson's heretical inspiration, on fire with a spirit as they imagined what the future could bring, eager to get started, yet trembling with a vision of uncharted promises. In the same spirit of that momentous transition, I hope and pray that this collection of essays might also evoke in you feelings of passion and enthusiasm tempered with dedication and intention.

—Fredric Muir

ON THE TRINITY OF ERRORS

The lyrics to a popular song in one of our Unitarian Universalist hymnals asks three questions: "Where do we come from? What are we? Where are we going?" Knowing where we come from and what we are offer keys to answering the question of direction—after all, how can we know where we're going without a sense of where we've been? The last two sections of essays in this book answer the song's final question; this first group of authors addresses our history —where we have come from. What have been the guiding and shaping themes and principles of the last three centuries?

The lead essay in this section originated as the 2012 Berry Street Lecture, convened by the Unitarian Universalist Ministers Association, and was the impetus for this book. It calls out three errors that have significantly shaped our way of faith and its communities from the earliest years of our history—individualism, exceptionalism, and an aversion to authority. Each error has increasingly become an obstacle that undermines our future.

Tamara Lebak broadens the conversation on these errors by sharing insights and experiences from her ministry of "living under the collar" in Tulsa, Oklahoma (a reference to her experiment of wearing a traditional clergy collar when in public and the conversations it prompted). As part of these experiences, she names the tension that the errors have created for her—personally and professionally—and seeks some resolution by engaging others while acknowledging differences. If we can learn to be more open and not look past one another, then there is hope in challenging the errors. Thomas Schade furthers this examination by describing the relationship of James W. Fowler's "stages of faith" to the development of Unitarian Universalism's three errors. This essay brings clarity and resolution to the question, Where did we come from?

How Unitarian Universalism's errors have generated a confusing story, especially for those whose place of origin is not the United States, is the theme of Parisa Parsa's essay. She examines how our faith's theology and spirituality and way of doing church are so deeply rooted in the errors of European American liberal religious culture that for an outsider it is a foreign story and far from welcoming. She reaches bold and challenging conclusions. Cheryl M. Walker's essay also recalls experiencing the US cultural story as an outsider—as an African American and a child of the Nation of Islam. She recollects the comfort, safety, and stability of the teachings of the collective, qualities not found in Unitarian Universalism with its emphasis on individualism. She looks forward to a day when community and individualism can be balanced.

Finally, our faith's allergy to authority is the topic of Kimberly Wildszewski's essay. A birthright Unitarian Universalist, she shares her story of church and faith—and now her ministry—and how these were shaped by Unitarian Universalism's subtle and overt narratives about authority that she heard and continues to hear.

Unitarian Universalism's attachment to the trinity of individualism, exceptionalism, and a resistance to authority will not take us where we want and need to go. It's a new day, and as these essayists show, the nineteenth- and twentieth-century tenets of our liberal faith have become errors—they are misguiding, corrupting, and narrowing.

The iChurch Revealed

FREDRIC MUIR

Faith is always evolving, changing, in transition—as is life. Whether it's our personal faith or the faith we call Unitarian Universalism, both are forever turning. Our beloved Unitarian Universalism has reached a turning point, a place of change with profound consequences that will determine whether there will be another generation of religious liberals who go by our name. In spite of the many bold and forward-thinking things that we do, in spite of the ministries to which we are committed, in spite of the marketing we have done, the picture of our congregations—their size, diversity, and style—has not changed much in the last two hundred, maybe even three hundred, years. The way we look, the way we *do* church, the way we think about ourselves, have stayed somewhat static. Statistics provide one indication of this: The number of people who claim Unitarian Universalism as their faith is growing smaller. No matter how you slant the data, our records tell us that we have remained either relatively unchanged for decades (if you use raw numbers) or we have shrunk considerably (if viewed as a percentage of the total US population). Either way, it does not look good; some might say it doesn't even look promising.

We should pay attention to what has happened to the Unitarian and Free Christian Churches of Britain, with whom we share considerable theological, intellectual, and cultural attributes. Their last century has been disheartening. At best, it appears that British

Unitarianism has another three generations before it dies. Their numbers tell the story:

- The largest congregation has 160 members.
- They have closed 50 percent of their churches in the last 80 years.
- The average congregation has 15 members.
- In 2010, the total number of Unitarians in Great Britain was 3,690.

While our British friends tell us how hard it is to get accurate numbers, accuracy is really not the issue. The issue is that their church is on the downward slide of the tipping point and there is no turning it around. All this in spite of familiar-sounding attributes that should make for a bright future: a ministry and assembly of congregations deeply committed to justice making; an increasingly multicultural and diverse society from which to grow; an outstanding history replete with culture-shaping luminaries; all the resources necessary for a stable and thriving religious faith (that is, professional ministry, property, and wealth). One of their leaders shared with me that in his lifetime they will likely become a minuscule community of faith with enormous riches (from bequests and the sale of property). But a vital and vibrant faith and church will be gone.

Here are a few of the questions I have for Unitarian Universalists: Is the British Assembly the proverbial canary in the coal mine for other Unitarian Universalists? While the assembly has passed the tipping point with little likelihood of revitalization, how far are we North Americans from teetering on this point? How far are we from tipping? Have we—will we—lose control of our future? A perfect storm is taking shape and pushing us to the tipping point, events forcing us to address these questions. "There's a change a-comin'" that we have all read about; we have seen it in the making. A confluence of events is taking shape, the effects of which we are late to recognize and absorb.

One of these events is described by the US Census, which projects that by 2043 our nation will be a majority minority nation, with minorities projected to constitute 57 percent of the population by 2060.[1] This means that we Unitarian Universalists, with our North Atlantic look—as reflected in our demographics, theology, and epistemology—will rapidly grow more cut off and isolated from the US population.

Another event described in research is hard to avoid, given its contrasting picture with the past. Whether your source is Gallup or Trinity College or the Pew Forum, that event is the rise of the "nones," many of whom are young adults claiming no religious affiliation, as in "none."

This perfect storm will have a transforming effect. The speed at which Unitarian Universalism has been downsizing will accelerate if only because our congregations will begin (and are) shrinking at an alarming rate. This might force us—if it's not already too late, and I believe it isn't—to step back and start afresh, renewed in a vision that is bold and well grounded. What's new about this picture is . . . well, honestly, there's not a lot that's new—believe me, we've heard it all! What is different is that we know the results of inaction, of not responding to the data and what we see.

Here's an irony: From Thomas Jefferson to Diana Eck[2]—with many in between—public figures have told Unitarian Universalists that we can be the religion of the future, not that we are, but that we can be. We have what it takes, it's been said, not only to weather the demographic challenges but also to welcome and grow from them and, in meeting twenty-first-century needs, sustain Unitar-

---

1   Charles Blow, "Race, History, a President, a Bridge," *New York Times*, March 9, 2015, A17.

2   In a letter to Dr. Benjamin Waterhouse, June 26, 1822, Thomas Jefferson wrote, "I trust that there is not a young man now living in the United States who will not die a Unitarian." In *Thomas Jefferson: Writings*, ed. Merrill D. Peterson (New York: Library of America, 1984), 1458–59. Religious scholar Diana Eck delivered the installation sermon for Rev. Galen Guengerich at All Souls Church, New York City, on October 28, 2007, in which she said, "You are, in my estimation, the church of the new millennium."

ian Universalism for generations to come.

What those declaring our bright future have not told us is that in order to be this twenty-first-century religion, we must create significant change, changes over which—unlike the demographic challenges—we *do* have control. Fundamental to our survival is a paradigm shift, a frame bending that goes deep into the history, character, and epistemology of Unitarian Universalism and its members, because it goes to the essence of how we understand and see ourselves and, in turn, relate to the world at large, which means how we relate to our demographic context. Fundamental to our future is recognizing that our way of faith, from its leadership to its Sunday service to justice-making partnerships, has been supported and nurtured by a trinity of errors, leading not only to ineffectiveness but also to an inability to share our liberating message. That is to say, while Unitarian Universalism's gospel is good news, it is losing its vitality and relevance.

The trinity is this:

- We are being held back and stymied by a persistent, pervasive, disturbing, and disruptive commitment to individualism that misguides our ability to engage the changing times.

- We cling to a Unitarian Universalist exceptionalism that is often insulting to others and undermines our good news.

- We refuse to acknowledge and treat our allergy to authority and power, though all the symptoms compromise a healthy future.

These three organizing and corrupting narratives have shaped our story. Naming and addressing these issues and the results will be rewarding, meaningful, and terribly challenging—and for some unthinkable and impossible. I have characterized this change as moving from iChurch to Beloved Community.

How Unitarian Universalism arrived at this place of frame-bending decision making is not unlike the personal stories we've heard from the thousands who have either remained Unitarian Universalist or left another path to become Unitarian Universalist. My story is not terribly different. Here's what happened: As a child, I loved church. My Disciples of Christ congregation felt liberal; its ministers were thoughtful and progressive. When Don Wheat, who later became the parish minister at Third Unitarian Church, was called, my spirit and his connected, and I felt nudged toward ministry. That was in sixth grade. Theology, spirituality, and ecclesiology were immaterial to me; I loved our congregation and by high school was responding to the call to ministry.

Later, on April 22, 1970, near the end of my junior year in college, the "something happening here" that wasn't "exactly clear," came into focus at 2 p.m. That day was the first Earth Day, and I was in a class on American Transcendentalism; we were reading Emerson, Thoreau, and Whitman. We convinced our professor to hold class outside on that beautiful spring day. We pleaded with him: Emerson, we told him, would approve! We sat in the grass and listened as he leaned against a large shade tree and read aloud Emerson's "The Divinity School Address." It was as though he was channeling the Sage of Concord and speaking to me.

After class, I asked what religion Emerson was. Unitarian, he said. I asked if it still existed. "Exist?" he replied. "Yes, it exists! There's a congregation on the west side. I'm a member. Do you want to go Sunday?" And that was that.

I cannot emphasize enough just how transforming the Address and other works of "Saint" Emerson were for me; they moved me and set me in a new direction. Benjamin Anastas critiques Emerson's imprint on American identity, primarily his essay "Self-Reliance," and captures how I felt for years:

> This is the essay's greatest virtue for its original audience:
> it ordained them with an authority to speak what had been
> reserved for only the powerful, and bowed to no greater
> human laws, social customs or dictates from the pulpit.
> "Trust thyself: every heart vibrates to that iron string." Or:

"No law can be sacred to me but that of my nature." Some of the lines are so ingrained in us that we know them by heart. They feel like natural law.[3]

Prior to my Earth Day epiphany, I was religious but not spiritual, because I never had the words to put to the spirituality I had known since childhood. Emerson provided what I needed to be both religious and spiritual. As I said earlier, my story is not unique; thousands of us can tell these kinds of stories.

As the patriarch of American Transcendentalism, Emerson contributed to shaping twentieth-century ideology and the story Americans tell about ourselves. That story is about American uniqueness and individualism and has been expressed in myriad ways. One of those has relevance to the title of this essay. Several years ago I wondered what the *i* placed in front of Apple product names means. I found two explanations: One said that the *i* means "Internet"; the other said that the *i* stands for "individual," as in one's own personal, individual piece of technology to be used for whatever purpose you want, to help you "Think Different" (which was Apple's tagline). The theme of individualism was creatively and appealingly exploited in Apple's commercial, a Kerouac-like celebratory homage to Emersonian individualism:

> Here's to the crazy ones. The misfits. The rebels. The troublemakers. The round pegs in the square holes. The ones who see things differently. They're not fond of rules. And they have no respect for the status quo. They push the human race forward.[4]

Individualism shaped not only American culture writ large but also Unitarian Universalism: We comprise the church of Emersonian individualism; we are the iChurch. I'm not sure Emerson's

---

3 Benjamin Anastas, "The Foul Reign of Emerson's 'Self-Reliance,'" *The New York Times Magazine*, December 2, 2011.
4 Many websites offer a full discussion and viewing of the commercial. Search for "the crazy ones commercial."

goal was for us to be "the crazy ones," but Unitarian Universalist church historian Conrad Wright argues that the result was "the disintegration of institutional religion [because] one cannot build a church on Emerson's dicta: 'men are less together than alone,' or 'men descend to meet.'" Wright concludes, "For both Emerson and Parker, a true community is not painfully constructed by people who have struggled to learn how to live together, but is made up of atomic and unrelated individuals."[5]

I am not an Emerson scholar, so I cannot say with authority, but let's pretend, if only for the moment, that Wright's view is wrong. I have read enough of Emerson to feel certain that he celebrated the gifts of individuality, the beauty of nature's differences and diversity, of which humans are a part. We, as a nation and as a religious community, took the blessing and joy of individuality and made it an ideology, made it a theology, and did a bad job of making it polity. We went from individuality to individualism and ended where, as Wright convincingly argues, Emerson took us: the demise of institutional religion.

While individualism may have been a bold and appealing way to create and build a nation and its institutions and to grow Unitarian Universalism (it might have felt even natural or God-given), it is not sustaining: Individualism will not serve the greater good, a principle to which we have committed ourselves. Little to nothing about the ideology and theology of individualism encourages people to work and live together, to create and support institutions that serve common aspirations and beloved principles. This was a way of dreaming and living before the storm.

Unitarian Universalists have been telling two stories, only one of which will deepen and grow our future. One of those stories, the one with which we lead, is from the Transcendentalists and is captured and articulated in the shadow side of our Principles. When used as an expression of individualism rather than an expression

---

5 Conrad Wright, "Unitarian Universalist Denominational Structure," in *Walking Together: Polity and Participation in Unitarian Universalist Churches* (Boston: Skinner House Books, 1989), 86–87.

of the joy and celebration of individuality, the Principles come dangerously close to sounding like an ideology or creed turned theology and spirituality.

Buried under the vision in our Principles, weighted down by the many sources that inspire our living tradition, as though it was a footnote, we find a second story captured in a sentence few ever get to or read, one that speaks to what will sustain and grow us. It is not the language of individualism, not of the iChurch, but of covenant: "As free congregations we promise to one another our mutual trust and support."

We cannot do both covenant and individualism; individuality yes, but not individualism. I've heard it suggested that we should begin our Principles with "respect for the interdependent web"—that is, with a broader view than just the "inherent worth and dignity of every person." I suspect that this change wouldn't go over well, because people know that living as a community in covenant is too hard, as if to suggest that individualism comes so easily because it's natural: Therefore it must be right! Articulating and living our Principles as a commitment to covenant, creating and sustaining a community by "promising to one another our mutual trust and support," takes extra effort.

Besides its misleading theology and spirituality, individualism creates and supports two related obstacles that prevent the promise of covenant. One of these obstacles is Unitarian Universalist exceptionalism. Given our faith's parallel development with the nation, our proclivity to exceptionalism is no surprise. Law professor Randall Kennedy describes American exceptionalism. Using his words with a slight adaptation, here is how the Unitarian Universalist version of exceptionalism sounds to many: Unitarian Universalism is a faith shaped by "perceptions, ideas, intuitions, and ambitions which posits, among other things, that [our way of religion] is uniquely virtuous, uniquely powerful, uniquely destined to accomplish great things, and thus uniquely authorized to act in ways to which [Unitarian Universalists] would object if done by other [ways of faith]."[6] While there was an era in which Unitarian Universalist exceptionalism was robustly preached, today few among us would ever be caught speaking the dialect of exceptionalism; yet it gets spoken frequently in an indirect manner. Whether as a source of pride, personal and community truth, embellishment, anger, clarification, or, strangely enough, welcoming—we hear the inflection of Unitarian Universalist exceptionalism from the pulpit, from newcomer's classes, from Sunday greeters, from those who are earnestly trying to explain our way of religion to the uninformed. As unique as our experience with Unitarian Universalism may be, it is not the only way. We must stay conscious of how we explain, defend, or share, lest we come across as elitist, insulting, degrading, isolating, even humiliating to others. The iChurch's exceptionalism is a barrier to sharing the good news of Unitarian Universalism.

Another obstacle shaped by the iChurch is our allergy to power and authority, which often results in its misuse and abuse. Our personal and institutional pasts give some insight into this issue. We have many reasons to be suspicious of hierarchical structures. Our histories have found us under the heel of systems of authority. Many of us left faith communities where no room was made for different views or disagreements. Our institutional and personal pasts explain why we take inspiration from Emerson's powerful words on the sanctity of the individual: "Whoso would be a man must be a nonconformist. . . . Nothing is at last sacred but the integrity of your own mind. . . . Absolve you to yourself and you shall have the suffrage of the world."[7] As a college junior, these words were radical and empowering to me; I was at an age and place when I needed to hear Emerson's counsel. Now I see that what was good for me would not have been healthy for institutional growth and stability, not then and not now. Conflating

---

6 Randall Kennedy, *The Persistence of the Color Line: Racial Politics and the Obama Presidency* (New York: Pantheon Books, 2011), 192.
7 Ralph Waldo Emerson, "Self-Reliance," in *Selections from Ralph Waldo Emerson*, ed. Stephen E. Whicher (Boston: Riverside Editions, 1960), 147.

the narrow path of individualism with the promise of institutional health is a misleading formula we have been using for at least two centuries, a formula that gets played out regularly in our congregations. Benjamin Anastas describes what may sound like a familiar scenario with sardonic and prickly words:

> The larger problem . . . has been Emerson's tacit endorsement of a radically self-centered worldview. It's a lot like the Ptolemaic model of the planets that preceded Copernicus; the sun, the moon and the stars revolve around our portable reclining chairs, and whatever contradicts our right to harbor misconceptions—whether it be Birtherism, climate-science denial or the conviction that Trader Joe's sells good food—is the prattle of the unenlightened majority and can be dismissed out of hand.[8]

Unitarian Universalism's allergy to and misuse of power and authority is a factor in our inability or unwillingness to welcome and listen to a diversity of interests and passions, without being distracted and immobilized, and then move forward, promising "our mutual trust and support" for the common good while walking as a community with space for those who disagree. Failure at this contributes to our inability to grow and deepen and shape a healthy future. In those UU congregations where the antidote to the allergy has been found and administered, where a clear and deep understanding addresses the potential of abuse and misuse of authority and power, those congregations are among our most vibrant, growing, and electric.

Promising our mutual trust and support is not easy, and the challenges of the iChurch are not new. These barriers were factors at the 1865 organizing meeting of the National Conference of Unitarian Churches. Conrad Wright notes, "The resulting tensions continued for a full generation or more. To this day, they remain

---

8 Anastas, "Foul Reign."

imperfectly reconciled."[9] The proponents of the iChurch eventually won the day, and the trinity of challenges and the barriers they created were ingrained; they have ossified.

If individualism led us to the iChurch, then covenant can shape the Beloved Community, where the promise of individuality and justice inspire, empower, broaden, and deepen all. *Beloved community* was popularized by Rev. Martin Luther King Jr. The phrase was authored by Josiah Royce, a scholar familiar to King's teachers at Boston University School of Theology, where King completed his doctoral work. Church Historian Gary Dorrien writes,

> For Royce and the personalists [the Beloved Community] expressed the ethical meaning of the kingdom of God. King taught that the foundation of the beloved community is the divine indwelling that equally graces all people: "There is no graded scale of essential worth; there is no divine right of one race which differs from the divine right of another. Every human being has etched in his personality the indelible stamp of the creator."[10]

Rev. Shirley Strong elaborates on King's vision: "I understand the term Beloved Community to mean an inclusive, interrelated society based on love, compassion, responsibility, shared power, and a respect for all people, places, and things—a society that radically transforms individuals and restructures institutions,"[11] which is to say Beloved Community is shaped by what we know and feel as justice.

Unitarian Universalism has arrived at an epistemology opportunity, a breakthrough moment, where we must write a new nar-

9   Conrad Wright, "Associational Proliferation and Bureaucratic Development, 1865–1898," in *Congregational Polity: A Historical Survey of Unitarian and Universalist Practice* (Boston: Skinner House Books, 1997), 68.
10   Gary Dorrien, *Social Ethics in the Making: Interpreting an American Tradition* (Hoboken, NJ: Wiley-Blackwell, 2009), 394.
11   Shirley Strong, "Toward a Vision of Beloved Community," The Chaplaincy Institute, February 2007, http://chaplaincyinstitute.org/library/spirituality-and-social-justice/toward-a-vision-of-beloved-community.

rative. Ivone Gebara says that "epistemology is nothing more than an invitation to think about how we know ourselves and the things that surround us in our everyday lives."[12] We have an urgent need for what Jacqueline Lewis calls "storying," which means telling, writing, and living the story of who we will be, who we are becoming.[13] We must say and live how it is we want to know ourselves and the Unitarian Universalist story we want others to know, an epistemology that has, as all knowing does, ethical and justice consequences.

The vision of a deep covenantal community life as named in our Principles is bold, and many of us recite our Principles with passion and pride as we testify, march, or speak with newcomers. It is vital that we commit to this expression of our faith not as iChurch, not from the narrow goal of individualism, but as the promise of covenant and Beloved Community. The Unitarian Universalist story for the twenty-first century begins not only with our historical commitment to social justice outreach but also with congregational justice inreach; it begins with the congregation you attend. Don't you see that your congregation is the Beloved Community? This is a complex challenge with a deeper explanation.

For five years, I was a UUA Empowerment Workshop trainer. Two members from the team of trainers would be assigned to a congregation who wanted to be more deliberate in their justice-making ministry. We would arrive with possibilities for several workshops built on their goals. Every congregation with which I worked said they wanted more engagement in the larger community; they were all about working for change "out there," in the world around them. Not once did a congregation believe they had to change, that they might become a model of what they were seeking, that they could become the Beloved Community. This is not surprising, since this is not how the iChurch works.

---

12 Ivone Gebara, *Longing for Running Water: Ecofeminism and Liberation* (Minneapolis: Fortress Press, 1999), 20.
13 Jacqueline J. Lewis explores this in *The Power of Stories: A Guide for Leading Multi-Racial and Multi-Cultural Congregations* (Nashville: Abingdon Press, 2008).

How often I have heard from those I serve—in my own congregation and in others too—that "we spend too much time and
money on ourselves. We need to get out in the community and
do more!" Yes, we need to do more. And how convenient to want
to reform the world, because the work of shaping and modeling
our congregations as Beloved Communities, not as the iChurch,
means addressing the challenges of individualism, exceptionalism,
and authority.

There is an urgency to telling our story of covenant and Beloved
Community. The storm is passing over, and who will we be on the
other side of it? For most of Unitarian Universalist history, we have
lived the story of the iChurch, which birthed an ecclesiology that
sacralized individualism, and not surprisingly, our congregations
have not flourished. Knowing ourselves as Beloved Communities
is a story the world awaits, and if not the world, then at the very
least, those who ache and yearn for what we can be. The storm is
like a significant weather event a meteorologist begins predicting
days before it is upon us, urging us to prepare, yet many simply
ignore the warnings because they're convinced they will remain
unscathed. There are many reasons to welcome and embrace its
lasting and shaping consequences. To feel its revitalization and
regeneration in order to broaden and deepen our way of faith will
take preparation and effort. "Now is the accepted time," W. E. B.
Du Bois reminds us. "Not tomorrow, not some more convenient
season. . . . It is *today* that we fit ourselves for the greater usefulness
of tomorrow."[14]

---

14 W. E. B. Du Bois, *Prayers for Dark People*, ed. Herbert Aptheker (Amherst:
University of Massachusetts Press, 1980), 36.

Living "Under the Collar" with Unitarian Universalism

TAMARA LEBAK

I recently began a social experiment to explore the intersection of my two very different professional roles of minister and change management consultant. I started wearing a clerical collar. Ministers in the Unitarian Universalist tradition wear clerical collars only on special occasions, if ever. Mostly we just blend in. People don't know what we do for a living unless they see us at church, they ask, or we offer. I decided to wear the uniform of ministry every day except Sunday for a year to learn about myself, my church, and those with whom I share a city. I wanted to be forced to grapple with what the collar means to me and to engage more with others about what it means to them.

Wearing a collar means there is no question about my profession. And wearing it in Oklahoma as a woman and a member of the LGBTQ community, I am a walking example of difference. I wondered, When does wearing a collar ease my interactions and when does it get in the way? How does the collar hide my identity and how does it expose it? Where do I fit in in the ministry and where do I push the boundaries? How would turning up the volume on my ministerial identity change me?

For the most part, my experiment is pretty simple: Day to day I simply go about my business and do what most people do, I just do it in a collar. I've changed two flat tires, been pulled over for speeding, attended Twelve-Step meetings, and gotten (another) tattoo. For the most part it has made me hyper aware of being me . . . in my collar. But I have also stretched even what I thought was possible in a collar by recording my first solo album and winning a poker tournament (all for the cause). I've been writing about my experience in a blog called "Under the Collar in Oklahoma."

Living "under the collar" has helped me live into the separate pieces of myself. It has helped me bring together my various identities that used to feel so disparate and has created an opportunity for me to talk with others about them. By embracing my religious identity, I can be part of conversations that otherwise would have not been possible.

Most people have been very nice during my experiment. They have focused only on what we have in common as a way to build connection and to reduce discomfort or conflict. I have found myself doing that as well. Across our diverse society we've learned to do this as a way to get along. Yet, consequently, we leave little room for difference.

My experiment has taught me several lessons: To be an effective leader I need to be *more* of who I am and not less. To arrive at the most creative responses to problems, I must strike a balance between being an individual and being a member of the community, between differentiating and joining. When I model sharing complexity—when I differ from the group yet stay at the table and honor the connection—I create a culture in which others can do the same.

In 2010 I was introduced to the Developmental Model of Intercultural Sensitivity (DMIS), a scale made up of stages of the ways we encounter cultural differences. People and organizations are plotted along a continuum from denial to defense to minimization to acceptance to adaptation to integration.

According to Milton Bennett, the creator of the scale, when you plot people and organizations on the scale, it forms a bell curve, with the majority falling into the minimization stage. This means that most people focus primarily on sameness and minimize differences. The differences they are able to recognize are only those that do not require more than a surface-level relationship.

The dominant culture highly values minimizing differences so that we can accomplish a common task or so that we can all just get along. Maybe you have said or heard statements like these, which reflect minimization:

"I don't see color."

"I don't think of you as black."

"You don't act gay."

"We just need to trust and respect each other"—often code for "You need to follow my rules so that we are not in conflict and so that I can trust you."

Minimization is in fact extreme individualism, because the rulers with which we measure the world are ourselves. We set ourselves up as the standard by which to experience all difference. To move from minimization to the next stage, we have to become aware of this paradox. We must come to understand the tools with which we measure the world, and how they came to be our tools, before we begin to examine the tools of others. By digging deeper into how we became who we are, we open ourselves up to see that others could have a completely different set of tools and experiences. Once we grasp our own complexity, we become ready to discuss with others their complexity, because we have something to offer them in return. Cultural curiosity without a foundation of self-understanding leads to a power imbalance, because we are asking others to reveal something about themselves that we cannot or have not explored in ourselves.

Also according to the research of the DMIS, there are appropriate interventions along the developmental continuum. For example, in the polarization stage, where we see the world primarily in categories of us and them, the way to move to the next stage is to focus on commonality. When you have mastered the skill of focusing on commonality you arrive at the next stage: acceptance. However, focusing too much on commonality can keep us stuck in minimization.

We do unto and for others as we think they want done unto or for them, without really being in relationship with them. Until we do the self-analysis required of us, we don't even know what we are missing.

Articulating our own cultural complexity as a way to move from minimization to acceptance feels counterintuitive. My experiment living under the collar felt that way at first too. But it is helping me to differentiate myself while remaining engaged.

We need to learn to see the culture that we are a part of and to articulate how we identify with or differentiate from it. Then we can stand up against that with which we do not identify and champion those things that we believe are valuable. Self-exploration could be the key to ending oppression and changing our racial landscape. At All Souls in Tulsa, doing the work of racial caucusing alongside the study of intercultural competency is transforming the congregation.

This kind of cultural exploration involves asking questions like these: How did you come to understand your concepts of trust and respect, love and justice? Who are your models of authority and power, and how do you interact with them? What do leaders do and how are they "supposed to" act? And especially, What did your family teach you about race?

When you are white like me (or appear that way, and so receive white privilege) you have to do a lot of diving to understand the water you are swimming in. Whiteness is a cultural-historical construct, and learning more about how it came to be and why will challenge us. Until we understand our own culture, we will stay in minimization and likely even get thrown back into the previous stage of polarization when under stress. We need to learn more about who we are, make space for difference, and understand our own resistance styles and those of others.

Addressing the challenges of individualism is an example of the cultural self-exploration that Unitarian Universalist churches need to do in order to escape the constraints of minimization and move to acceptance and eventually adaptation. We must examine "what is" and "how things are done around here," and what has yet to be reconstructed in our movement. Otherwise we will continue to miss out on the glorious diversity and complexity of the human experience and remain paralyzed by our own internal resistance. Our uncompromising commitment to individualism continues to get in our way. Unitarian Universalist culture magnifies the individual to the sacrifice of our mission. How many of us have been in a meeting that was thwarted by a personal agenda? We are being stymied by internal arguments about our collective identity and by the tyranny of the minority. Our leaders are thrown off course by personal agendas that do not fit the mission or vision of the collective. Ministers are frozen in their tracks by resistance. To counter the ideology of individualism, we need a theology of change.

My own theology of change is grounded in the work I have done at All Souls (Tulsa)—corporate executive coaching and organizational development consulting, which I call the quarter turn. When we are actively seeking to influence a system, we must be in relationship. This requires recognizing "what is" for the other person or the institution. Once there is agreement about that, I can then work to expose a new cultural concept that is only one quarter of a turn from any current position. A full turn and the participants will not go with me at all. Three-quarters of a turn and I will leave the majority behind and polarize a significant portion. A half turn can be done successfully on occasion but requires me to cash in all my political chips and may slow progress on the next change initiative. A quarter turn offered in the relational context of a mutual goal builds a new foundation from which the work may be continued.

When we are in the business of being change agents, it behooves us to not only identify resistance but also seek it out and address it constructively. When resistance is seen as a natural part of the change process, we are able to work with the energy instead of allowing it to derail us or prevent progress. I often tell leaders that resistance shows that the resistor cares about the issue. More undermining than resistance is apathy or silence. If we do not know where the resistance is, then we do not have an adequate snapshot of "what is." Without that we will not be able to move forward from sure footing.

Leading requires understanding ourselves as change agents. It involves knowing the impact we have, teaming up with those who have skill sets we do not, and knowing whether we are the right messenger for the message. Change comes from leaders leading from who they are and where they are, grounded in their own story and the narrative of the church. For example, I may not be the right person to lead a congregation on LGBTQ issues, because to those whose ideas I would like to change it may appear self-serving. They might not hear me in the same way that they could hear my straight, white male colleague and ally. We can effect more change when we lean into being effective over simply being right.

While living "under the collar" and learning about the ways I differentiate and cooperate, I have discovered more of the complexity in who I am. By leading with an identity that used to be mostly invisible, I am able to have conversations that I otherwise would not have had about what it means to be me and to be a minister. My biggest takeaway from this experiment so far is that having biases is not actually the problem. The problem is when our biases are invisible to us and we react instead of act.

What are the uniforms of your culture that you don't even know you are wearing? I invite you to spend the energy and the time learning how you came to be who you are. Define your values and your commitments and then bring your whole self to the table. The more we are able to understand our assumptions and demonstrate the complexity of our own identities, the less we will be threatened by the differences of others and the more accepting we all will be. Rather than an argument for individualism, this is a call for an in-depth study of our own culture as it manifests in us. Our self-examination provides a foundation for building relationships that make more room for difference.

You may have concluded, as I have, that the challenges we face are not unique to our personal or institutional lives. They are so much bigger. Many of the problems facing our country and our world today are, in fact, primarily religious in nature, clashes of constructs that keep us separate and feuding, fueled by fundamentalism and an "othering" worldview. If we are to change this religious landscape, Unitarian Universalists must be in relationship with the decision makers. We must stop marginalizing ourselves out of the religious conversation. The first step is to admit our own fundamentalisms. Our ideology that rejects religious language and experience and remains committed to individualism, exceptionalism, and a resistance to authority is curtailing our power to influence the religious landscape in America.

I pray that we lead the way from our spheres of influence to engage in a religious dialogue grounded in who we are and where we would like to go. I believe we are perfectly poised to do so, if we would just get out of our own way.

Unitarian Universalist
Faith Development in Stages

THOMAS SCHADE

Are Unitarian Universalists wedded to an unholy trinity of individualism, exceptionalism and a resistance to authority that will lead us into oblivion? Does the precarious position of the Unitarians of Great Britain warn us of what church failure could look like?

The unholy trinity is the remnant of an obsolete story that we tell about ourselves. In that story we are a band of rebellious freethinkers, cantankerous and difficult to manage—the kind of people to whom the cliché "like herding cats" applies. They attend what Fredric Muir calls, in the first essay of this book, the "iChurch"—the "i" standing for "individual."

In reality though, we are living a different story now; we are trying, in our way, to build congregations that foreshadow the Beloved Community. Our thinking is still iChurch, but our practice is more Beloved Community than we think. We need to write this new story that illuminates the Beloved Community as our shared goal. We need to question the role that individualism plays as a defining value of the Unitarian Universalist story.

Muir contrasts individualism with individuality. The former is an ideology or theology that overvalues individuals and their perceptions, while the latter is a healthy personal trait. If personal self-expression is often positive, while individualism is not, how does that relate to the process of group faith development?

The faith development of individuals is inter-related with the development of their surrounding communities through a complicated process. James W. Fowler's *Stages of Faith* (1981) offers a valuable way to understand faith development as a series of stages that correspond with stages of a person's overall development through the life cycle. The move from iChurch to Beloved Community provides a clarifying model. Fowler describes faith development as a process of evolving relationships between individuals and their communities. It is this relationship that Muir has identified as being stuck. Fowler describes six stages of faith development, but I will focus only on the last four stages, which progress roughly from middle-school age through mature adulthood. Even the names Fowler gives the stages refer to the relationship between the individual and the community in the formation of that faith stage.

Synthetic-Conventional Faith is when people, usually at a younger age, adopt the faith stance of their surrounding community. They think, "This is who we are and this is what we believe and this is how we should act." It is faith as identity with a group.

People who were childhood converts, or cradle Unitarian Universalists, did this work of building a faith identity within Unitarian Universalism—at worship, in religious education programs, and in their homes.

Many Unitarian Universalists in this stage of faith development do not associate Unitarian Universalism with freedom of thought. Some say, "Unitarian Universalism is an identity, not a dogma or set of beliefs."

In the stage of Synthetic-Conventional Faith, faith development occurs as the person absorbs community beliefs and values. In the next stage, Individuative-Reflective Faith, the person develops an identity independent of the community. This can take many forms, but it often takes the form of conversion to a new faith.

Adult conversion often involves a process of individuation in which converts decide that their old religious life was not adequate for them, and they seek out a situation in which they can develop their own thoughts. In the past, Unitarian Universalism largely received new members from among people in this stage of their faith development. For many of them, what makes Unitarian Universalism attractive is its freedom of thought, its skepticism toward established Christian dogmas.

It should be no surprise, then, that a religion composed of many adult converts would value individuation. Unitarian Universalism has identified itself with the gesture of individual assertion: We are in love with Emersonian self-discovery.

Adult converts to Unitarian Universalism often tell stories of their moments of individuation: the recollection of the day they couldn't say the Nicene Creed anymore. They cherish their doubts and frame the task of faith development as "building your own theology"—the title of a widely used adult religious education program.

Further, Unitarian Universalists in this stage feel discomfort with proselytizing Unitarian Universalism. Any form of evangelism would impose on others' process of individuation. Some do not even put a high value on their children becoming Unitarian Universalists because children should have the same religious freedom that adults have exercised.

Other adult converts may revert to a previous stage of faith development after conversion, becoming interest in constructing a Unitarian Universalist identity based in the new Unitarian Universalist community. Perhaps the second of Muir's trinity of errors, Unitarian Universalist exceptionalism—what I would call UU sectarianism—is the expression of people redoing their earlier developmental work *after* becoming Unitarian Universalist. Gestures toward building a Unitarian Universalist identity can be seen in an attachment to things that are particular to our faith tradition: the chalice, the seven Principles, the water and flower communions, our logos and coffee cups and T-shirts. These are who we are. These are all markers of a previous stage of faith development.

At the stage of Conjunctive Faith, the Unitarian Universalist gestures include the claim that Unitarian Universalism is a multifaith movement with a deep interest in world religions and a desire to honor every spiritual path while avoiding misappropriation. Comments such as "there are many paths up the same mountain" and "the same light shines through different windows" both express Conjunctive thought, as do worship art and symbols that include all the world religions. In this stage, thinking flows directly from where previous individualizing thinking left off. If my faith development consists only of distinguishing what I believe from what others believe, I will end up with no religious community.

The attitudes of Conjunctive Faith have been crucial in recent Unitarian Universalist history. The insights from that approach got us out of the humanist versus theist conflict that had paralyzed our theological development. It gave us the tools to build a worshipping community that included believers and non-believers.

But Conjunctive Faith thinking has its own pitfalls, including a paralyzing relativism. Some young adults who leave Unitarian Universalism say that there is "no there there"—all they have seen is tolerance and respect for other religions, but little original religious content.

Fowler is appropriately modest in describing the normative end stage of his system of faith development, Universalizing Faith. In this stage, one transcends some of the contradictions of the previous stage.

The transition to Universalizing Faith involves overcoming the paradox of individual and universal apprehensions. This stage becomes a disciplined, activist incarnation, making real and tangible the imperatives of absolute love and justice.

The most elusive language in Unitarian Universalism is the one that describes the personal transformation that is the object and goal of UU faith development. In our aversion to authority—the third of the trinity of errors—we do not give our religious leaders the authority to verbalize where they are leading us, even though we hunger for their inspiration.

It's important to set this development into historical context. During the rise of conservative culture in the United States (1968–2008), the culture of individuation as defining Unitarian Universalism started to break up. As far as I can see, the impetus came from the religious educators. Parents were reporting that our UU children felt anxious and unsafe because they could not defend their family's religious affiliations to more conservative friends. Our children needed to know that Unitarian Universalism is "a real religion."

While Unitarian Universalist adult converts may have skipped the stage of group identification (Synthetic-Conventional Faith) in their Unitarian Universalist faith development, their children could not. They needed to know who we are, what we believe. To meet this need, UU religious education began to focus on developing a Unitarian Universalist identity.

Now some of those children of the Nixon-Reagan-Bush era are becoming our ministers. Many of that generation did not remain active in Unitarian Universalist congregations (another subject), but we are most influenced by those who stayed. Many have grown up in Unitarian Universalism, and know it as their religion, who they are, and what they believe. However their process of individuation occurred, it did not take them away from Unitarian Universalism.

To them, Unitarian Universalism has always been Beloved Community and many are frustrated by the iChurch attitudes they see as still dominant among older Unitarian Universalists. Muir, who is a sensitive elder, gets it and wants us to move on. And I can understand why. But, as much as that individual self-assertion seems to be in our way, as we work on building the Beloved Community, we cannot forget how crucial that step in faith development is for many people. They experience a moment when what the world assumes them to be rubs up against the person they are discovering they really are.

That external expectation has so many forms: It can be the box of a racial or ethnic stereotype. It can be a resource denied because of the part of town a person lives in, or the school a person attends. It can be the cold, indifferent assumption that people like them are used to suffering or being without health insurance or working for next to nothing. It can be closer and even more personal than that:

the assumption of heterosexuality, even the assumption of gender and gender expression. It can be less severe: the assumption that people will always go to the same church that their family of origin did, or the surprise that friends express over someone wanting to worship at all. It can be the assumption that a well-paying job is everyone's highest goal. That external expectation can come from school, from church, and even from the people who love them most yet seem to know them the least.

The free expression of one's individuality is unfinished business for many of the world's people. Among the demographic most served by Unitarian Universalist congregations, there are many who have done this work and need to move on; but there are many others for whom it is personal work that still needs to be done.

Mary Oliver's great poem "The Journey" tells the story of someone leaving home, even though there are those who want her to stay to fix their lives. But she goes, and as she goes, she hears her own voice, perhaps for the first time. She has only one life, hers, and that is enough.

Or, as one song we frequently sing says: "If they say no, I'll go anyhow. I'm on my way. I'm on my way to the freedom land."

I believe that Unitarian Universalism would lose a vital piece of its soul if it loses touch with that moment of self-assertion when a person says, "No, I cannot stay here. I must leave. I must go my own way. Come with me if you can, but I will go alone if I have to."

Liberation and self-determination are sometimes hard, scary, and irreversible, but in many ways, they are indispensable steps in the process of spiritual growth. And if we are to love people and grow our congregations, we must reach out to everyone struggling with that first step.

Muir's critique of individualism is fairly narrow. He writes, "Individualism will not serve the greater good, a principle to which we have committed ourselves. Little to nothing about the ideology and theology of individualism encourages people to work and live together, to create and support institutions that serve common aspirations and beloved principles." Muir's critique is about how difficult it is to build community and institutions in an environment stuck in the stage of individuation.

Unitarian Universalist ministers and religious leaders have been frustrated for years by the habits of Muir's unholy trinity in our congregations: the half-hearted quality of people's commitment to our institutions; the unwillingness to share our good news, and the frustrations of being a religious leader to congregants who don't think they need one. But as frustrating as these are to Unitarian Universalist religious professionals, they are not really the obstacles that most of the world's people face at this time in their spiritual development. Religious communities are a means to faith development of the person and of the larger community, not just the end in itself. The problem with the ideology of individualism, the sectarian identity with Unitarian Universalism and the reflexive distaste for authority is not just that they prevent Unitarian Universalist growth in the coming storm. The problem is that they encourage self-centered and entitled human beings, people who are narrowly loyal to their clubs and unable to either lead or follow in the broader society. In short, our ideology sustains people in ways of living that are unhappy, unhealthy, and negative. It sustains people in feeling ill at ease in the world, uncomfortable with difference and themselves, and isolated and filled with an aggrieved sense of entitlement. There is a human cost to one-sided spirituality.

This is not the goal of the spiritual journey, no matter how one conceives of it.

We go on a spiritual journey to awaken in us a Deep Universalism, to transform our lives so that we embody human (and beyond) solidarity in a world divided by injustice and oppression. Deep Universalism is not sentimental and outside history but is engaged solidarity with those whose liberation is necessary for humanity, and the planet as a whole to advance. Deep Universalism is the discovery of the self, and the discovery of the self in relationship to the whole of humanity, the consciousness of Beloved Community. And it is the locating of the self in the present historical moment.

Universalism began as a particular Christian doctrine of salvation: that Jesus Christ saved all of humanity, not just an elect. As such, it was a radical reinterpretation of the Christian gospel. Within the Christian world, it is still disruptive, as those who speak and write about Deep Universalism have learned by losing their audiences and livelihoods. But Christian Universalism became less relevant after the rise of humanism. Once religious liberals no longer theologized within the framework of Christian systematic theology, Universalism lost its cutting edge.

Universalism took on a new relevance in the post-colonial world. Universalism evolved from being a Christian doctrine of salvation to be a more general theology of religion, one that asserted the essential unity and validity of all religious traditions. Those who embraced the Universalist spirit as a "religion of one world," as Universalist minister Kenneth Patton called it, are testaments of that development.

But there is little that is aspirational or inspirational about recognizing the validity of all the world's religions. It is a viewpoint, but it is not a practice. How does one go about it day to day? How does one worship? The material circumstances of the world today—transportation, communication, globalization—make a spirituality of global solidarity a more real goal than ever before.

The spirituality of Deep Universalism is the inner consciousness of the global Beloved Community. Deep Universalism is the articulation of Fowler's final stage of faith development: "a moral and ascetic actualization of the universalizing apprehensions. Heedless of the threats, . . . a disciplined, activist incarnation—a making real and tangible—of the imperatives of absolute love and justice. . . ."[1]

A popular Unitarian Universalist social action rallying cry is that we "stand on the side of love." Standing on the side of love is embodying a Deep Universalism, a spirituality of global solidarity. To be transformed in such a way is a journey with many steps and

---

1   James Fowler, *Stages of Faith: The Psychology of Human Development and the Quest for Meaning* (New York: Harper Collins, 1995), 200.

stages. It will not happen for many before the material conditions for it have been achieved: the communication and transportation systems that tie the world's people together. Deep Universalism is equally aware of both unities and diversities of cultures, and of the power dynamics that enmesh them. For the person, the path to Deep Universalism will move through times of self-assertion and times of submerging the self in larger communities. For many Unitarian Universalists, now is a time to grow past our excessive individualism; but that is not the whole journey.

Telling Our Story

PARISA PARSA

How do you tell the story of Unitarian Universalism?

Do you trace the lineage of ideas: of a God who is one rather than three, of a prophet who is more human than divine, of the divine present in each and all, of the salvation that is possible through a God of love? Do you skip stones through history as you introduce people to our faith—a faith of ideas, of possibilities, of heretics and martyrs? Do you start with Origen and Arius, stop to tell the fascinating tales of Michael Servetus and John Calvin, of Ferenc Dávid and King John, let everyone pause for a chuckle as you mention that the only time Unitarianism was a state-sanctioned religion was in Transylvania for a brief couple of years in the early sixteenth century, knowing they are picturing a minister in a Dracula cape with fangs and a little trickle of blood? And then the history gets closer and a little more possible to trace as a direct lineage, so you have to sort through which things of the many that light your own admittedly nerdy imagination you will choose to share: Will you talk about Faustus Socinus or go into more detail about Joseph Priestley? Will you intersect our story with that of the British crown and remind folks of the legacy of Henry VIII or focus instead on the ways the small Reformation house churches interpreted the gospel?

Whichever voyage you prefer, you'll need to bring your listeners safely to the shores of North America and tell the stories of the

arrival of the Puritans, where they will doubtless have mental pic-
tures of buckled hats and sour faces, of Hester Prynne and maybe
even Captain Ahab. If you're in a New England congregation, you
may be in a building built by Puritan hands, endowed with relics of
their industriousness and conquest, and so you'd best tell the story
especially carefully.

Further afield from New England, you can run as wild with
it as you wish or gloss over it with much more ease. The Pilgrims
were, after all, the people whose theology we rejected when in the
early nineteenth century we took up the name Unitarian and in
the mid-eighteenth century as Universalists we began to question
the exclusivity of salvation. Identifying with the heretics is easy
and feels so much more renegade and tough, doesn't it? You might
describe how the heresies continued onto more radical theological
paths, eventually abandoning the exploration of God altogether in
favor of comparative cosmology and ardent secular humanism—
all while we still claim to be a religious tradition, which just makes
it all the more delicious.

You may decide to make a passing mention of the practice of
covenant in Puritan congregations determined not to repeat the
sins of the Church of England. You might name the Cambridge
Platform as the source of our polity, and then posthumously pat
our forebears on their collective backs for renouncing salvation
only for the elect and the sole divinity of Jesus. We can celebrate
their belief in the possibility of moral improvement and point to
their charitable works, and there root our own passion for social
justice and our ardent work to honor inherent worth and dignity.

If you tell one of these stories, a mixture of them, or decide to
stay with something more personal, you can weave through them all
a powerful, liberal trinity of individualism, exceptionalism, and an
aversion to authority—attributes of liberal religion that have worked
well for many, especially in the United States. For some—for you?—
this trinity has been the lens through which orthodox religion has
been deconstructed while at the same time serving as the building
blocks with which personal faith has been reconstructed.

As we tell some version of this identity story, we are speaking the truth. But it would be just as truthful to start this story today, in your home setting. No matter what your context—whether your setting is urban, suburban, exurban, or rural, regardless of how far your journey toward wholeness has progressed—you can share from your mental file of images and experiences, things that you could not have made up if you tried! At times it can be challenging to remember exactly what about us and our neighbors is so wonderful, what keeps drawing us back in. But there is a truth about us that often brings us back, one that is the axis on which our faith's mission and future often turns: We try to balance ourselves. We often wonder, How do we plan the day when we're torn between the desire to save the world and the desire to savor it?

Tears have fallen, hearts have opened, souls have found comfort—ours included. This too is part of the story that must be told.

Here is still another part of the story: After the American Unitarian Association and the Universalist Church of America merged in 1961 to become the Unitarian Universalist Association, we have been striving to be relevant and to have a clear identity as a faith tradition. We have struggled with squaring our desire to be on the progressive, inclusive side of history with our identity as communities rooted in privilege. We have imagined in our communities and congregations the vision of the Beloved Community: the ideal place, the heaven on earth, the sacred kin-dom made real. And we have said in our congregations, "We can get there" in spite of—let's face it—our own misgivings. We've managed to say, "We can do this," when we've just been devastatingly disappointed and sometimes we've even talked ourselves back into that realm of hope and possibility by the time we're done. It's how we Unitarian Universalists save ourselves daily in this work.

And the story gets broader and deeper. Many of us have not a drop of that Puritan blood in us and trace our personal lineages to very different communities—something that will become increasingly so in Unitarian Universalist congregations. Yet for most of recent history, joining a Unitarian Universalist congregation has meant joining a culture of privilege and power, characterized by individualism, exceptionalism, and an aversion to authority, the "trinity of errors" that has shaped the Unitarian Universalist story for nearly three hundred years. Sharing in this culture, about which an increasing number of people know little, or from which they feel distant or at least uncertain, is often a problem. Yet the story we have often chosen to tell claims that we were always on the underside of history. In the words of TV's Stephen Colbert, we have chosen "truthiness" over truth, at least as it applies to our faith's lineage on this continent. It may be because we have been looking backward with our present values and rhetorical intent; it may be because we as a people are prone to identify with the underdog heroes of any story; it may be out of ignorance or just not caring to delve too deeply in the past when the future beckons us so urgently. Maybe for none of those reasons, maybe for all of them, we wrap ourselves in that vision like a clean, white shirt, and with a purity of intention and the fire of possibility we take up the work of getting there. We look around us at all that must change and feel the true sense of urgency about the task. People are suffering greatly in the gap between the right now and the not yet. And so we race off, feverishly pursuing that salvific goal of multicultural community that has erased racism and upends all oppression.

In our hurry to save the world, to figure out what we can do about what's past and make way for a better future, while immersed in a story shaped by errors, we have often done harm to ourselves and each other. In our fervent following after justice that has a particular shape we think we know, we lose our grounding in the spirit. With all the education we have about power and privilege and oppression and multiculturalism, we can't figure out why the work is still so hard. The world starts to divide into those who get it and those who don't. Those who are on the side of the good and right and true and those who are not. And if we don't feel as if we've done enough this month or this year, we're sure that everyone else is righteous and true, and we are ashamed of our inadequacy. If we are laboring under the weight of how hard we have tried and seeing no progress, indeed feeling invisible and ineffective for all our righteous work, we are quick and biting with our indictments of *those people* who just don't get it. The toughest judgments we have of others are only the tip of the iceberg of the tough talk we have for ourselves.

If I didn't know better, I'd think I came from Puritan stock.

Our Puritan roots were not what the church led with when my family came to Unitarian Universalism during my early teen years. We attended a church that had formed out of the fellowship movement, whose worship service consisted of a "concert and a book report," and, as far as I could tell, came from the minds of kindly male intellectuals wearing turtlenecks and blazers. My family was warmly welcomed in spite of—and I came to realize over time maybe in some ways *because of*—the oddities that kept us from feeling at home in other communities. My Iranian father was an academic, and with his brown skin and quirky accent quickly charmed everyone. And for his part he thought he was in heaven, talking about the events of the day with intelligent folks who also threw great potlucks. My parents threw parties with lots of Persian food, and all of their church friends would come over. After my dad had tried to coax the adventurous into tasting the eyeball of the lamb's head he used for a traditional Persian stew, we would settle in and enjoy the gyrations of a fellow congregant who was taking a belly-dancing class at the local community college.

It would never have occurred to us, nor do I think it occurred to anyone in the church, that by identifying ourselves as Unitarian Universalists we were tying our spiritual lineage to the Puritans, with attributes like individualism, exceptionalism, and anti-authoritarianism. We thought we were joining the faith of the heretics, not those who burned them. We were always the vanguard, never the killjoy rule followers! Our people weren't the Puritans, our people *split* from the Puritans.

The thing is, worldviews that shape us and have shaped our US culture don't just go away because we think our way out of them.

Even as the dissenters, our people were *for* those orthodox ideas before they were against them. Both Unitarians and Universalists gave up the notion of predestination centuries ago, and we still strive in so many ways to show ourselves among the visible saints: to look and act and think only of righteous things; to keep our clean shirts clean. And then to pity or chastise or deride those who have not met our standards, including ourselves.

Now that we have the Internet, there is really no limit to the places the Duke of Discomfort and the Dutchess of Fear can show up to haunt us. It's a habit that lives in the spiritual equivalent of our reptilian brains, taking over without warning when we're anxious. And we can never be good enough, because we readily take on the mark of shame for all that has been done before, and before before, and even before that. What's any one of us to do about what's been done? So hard to keep those clean shirts clean.

We could certainly go on as we have been, suppressing those judgments, and at best sitting quietly and stewing on them—at worst having them lash out with disproportionate force on some unsuspecting blogger or UUA staff member. We know how that looks and works. And we can still do all that while aspiring to a very different theology: worth and dignity affirmed, all are saved, interdependent web, always on a journey of growth, the holy is evolving with us . . . all those things we love to say. But wouldn't it be great to have some practices that help us shift our own internal conversation to start to match all those lofty aspirations? Wouldn't it be great to stop washing the dirt of the world from that shirt and lean into the good news of Universalism: that we are all already saved, all already good? What if we could take up the work of racial healing and true intercultural community building, fueled not by fear and shame and inadequacy but by the assurance of grace and genuine curiosity?

Our faith ancestors and their baggage are only part of the story, of course. They knew, perhaps far better than we, how challenging it could be to live with the specter of one's eternal salvation always at stake. And they knew it was not a solo proposition. They needed each other to interpret God's word for them and their lives and communities. They needed each other for forgiveness when they faltered. They needed each other to hold them to the worthiness of their striving. They needed something more than a trinity of errors; they needed Beloved Community; after all, they were gathered in covenant.

What the Puritans got right about this, and what we shy away from, is that the most meaningful covenant is the *double* covenant, between individuals in the community and between the community and God. We are accountable not just to each other, to some contract of agreement, but also to that journey of faith that can by its nature and by our indwelling nature transform us. Because when we walk faithfully together a sort of alchemy takes over, melting our stubborn hearts into greater wisdom, opening our stuck minds to the multiplicity of truth, moving us into greater harmony, not in opinion or experience but in spirit.

Covenant is the gift of leaning into each other's arms and together leaning into the Everlasting Arms: arms that hold and comfort and arms that also push us forward to take that next leap into justice. It all starts, though, with turning to our neighbor. It gains traction with our curiosity about their story. It gets deeper as we discover the subtler nuances of our own story. It goes the full monty when we together lay bare the pile of hurts along the way, and it clothes itself in glory when we find connection and healing and hope in new patterns of community that make space for us all.

Maybe the Beloved Community is just this practice, right here, right now, of encountering the holy in each other and striving and failing and loving and celebrating over and over again, finding new circles of practice beyond our own communities, and doing that over and over again.

There is no formula for this. There are not three steps or five or ten or twelve. There is just the steady journey of witnessing to the power of the good that dwells in us, pushing past our fears of failure by resting in the love that always already holds us. In that steady, ever-opening covenant lies the challenge and the joy of seeing and knowing the holy in each other, knowing that through our strife we are held by a larger love that has our backs, taking the time to name the miracle of our connection with ever greater awe.

How will you tell the story of your faith?

The Power of Community
and the Peril of Individualism

CHERYL M. WALKER

Sunday morning. My family and I are on our way to worship services. We walk the streets of Harlem, my brother and father in dark suits with bow ties; my sisters, my mother, and I dressed in white. The sea of people parts to let us pass; we are strong and confident, invulnerable. It is the early sixties and we are on our way to Muhammad's Mosque No. 7. We will meet others like us and greet each other with the familiar hand grasp, kiss, and blessings of "*as-salaam-alaikum*" (peace be unto you). We are powerful.

Our power comes from our collectiveness. Our power comes from being as one unit, dressed alike, sharing the same rituals, praying alike. Because we act as one we are able to build schools, publish newspapers, and start businesses. We have an unshakeable sense of who we are and are secure in our being. We are not like so-called Negroes, we are proud black women and men. It shields us from the racism that is pervasive in all other parts of our lives. We are not inculcated with a sense of inferiority; just the opposite, we have an unwavering sense of innate superiority. Our difference feels like a badge of honor, not one of shame.

Yet a shadow side exists. We are strong only if we are willing to conform. Individuality is discouraged. The rules are strict and there is no tolerance for breaking them. You cannot show up on Sunday morning wearing a red dress. Individuality is a willing acceptance of otherness, and there was no room for otherness. The price to pay for the power of this type of community is the loss of individuality. For some, me included, the price became too high, and so in my teenage years I made the choice to separate from the community; not from the faith but from the community, for I still loved many things about the faith of my childhood.

I kept my faith but lost my religion, because religion is always communal. You cannot be religious all by your lonesome. You can be spiritual but not religious. Religion is always communal, whereas being spiritual is an individual expression of faith. We create religion to find ways to express our spirituality in community. At times I very much missed the strength and security of being in a faith community where everyone prayed alike at the same time, in the same way, to the same God. And if being part of the Muslim community were only about prayer and food, I never would have left. But it was about so much more, so many more rules, so much conformity.

So I wandered the religious wilderness for many years, believing that I would never find a religious community where I could be me, just as I am. My story is not unique. Over the years I have met many a person wandering that same wilderness, giving up on ever finding a place their soul could call home. Like many of them, I tried other faith communities on for size, but none of them fit quite right. And what was the point of substituting one ill-fitting faith for another? I was wandering in the wilderness, until I was given a blessing by a dear friend.

The blessing she gave me was Unitarian Universalism. Invited to attend her church one Sunday, with a promise of a free lunch afterward (never underestimate the power of a free lunch), I went and found a seed of something. A second visit to another UU congregation and I saw the seed blossom. There in the pulpit was a black woman, the late Marjorie Bowens-Wheatley. I had never dreamed that there could or would be someone who looked like me in any pulpit. And her message spoke to me, all of me, my head, my heart, my spirit. But more than that, there were those banners.

If you have ever been in the sanctuary of the Community Church of New York, the first thing that gains your attention is the banners hanging from the rafters. They are six-foot banners representing some of the world's major religions. One of them was the familiar star and crescent of Islam. Without words, it spoke volumes about the religious freedom of this faith. It said what I had been thinking for a long time—each of these religions has something to teach us, yet not a single one of them has an exclusive ownership of the truth. In the front was a banner with a symbol unknown to me, a flaming chalice. It was not in the center, it was to the side, and that spoke volumes to me as well—even Unitarian Universalists don't have exclusive ownership of the truth. My spirit wept, I was home. These might just be my people. I could wear a red dress to worship on Sunday morning.

I fell in love with being an *individual* in a faith community. You mean I don't have to believe what I don't believe and that's okay? You're saying that I can be just who I am without leaving any part of me at home? You're telling me we don't all pray to the same God, in the same way, at the same time? What, you don't even have to believe in God? Really? My faith journey is my faith journey, not the one you've neatly mapped out for me? Get outta town! Where have you people been?

I was like a kid in a candy store. Me, me, me. My faith, my journey, my religion. It's all about me. This religion was created with me in mind, just waiting for the day that I would show up and make it complete. Thank you very much, all you people who came before me, whoever you were, for making a religion just for me. Of course I didn't say this, but I sure felt it. I could breathe again, I could sing, even if I didn't know any of the tunes—and I did read ahead to make sure I wasn't going to sing anything I didn't agree with.

I thought Unitarian Universalism offered me the ability to be in community without losing myself as an individual. This faith community would provide me with the safety and security to explore what I believed, not just what I didn't believe, with the hope of putting my beliefs into action to create tangible changes in my personal life and in the world. It offered me freedom. And I dove right in, headfirst into the refreshing waters of Unitarian Universalism.

Yet I also discovered a shadow side. There was no discipline of faith. It required little of me. All I had to do was sign a book and give some money and, *voila!*, I was a Unitarian Universalist. (I found out later that I didn't even have to give any money.) This group of people had no cohesion beyond a single congregation, and even within congregations there was little or no cohesion. Everyone had come thinking this religion was made just for them, even those people who had grown up in this faith. Therefore everyone thought everything should be for them. This wasn't individuality, it was individualism, worship of the individual.

While the childhood of my faith was powerful because of its strictness and conformity, Unitarian Universalism, by contrast, was weakened by its laxity and its individualism. With little or no allegiance to anything greater than, perhaps, a congregation, collectively we are unable to commit in the long term to transforming the world or even ourselves. There was no accountability for living our values, because we are hard-pressed (a) to state what they are and (b) to answer the question to whom or what are we all accountable.

While I loved this faith, and still do, I wondered about its people. It took a long time for me to decide to sign the membership book. I love the promise of this faith, but when I, as a person of color, look at us I wonder, How can we say we affirm our Principles and yet fail to accomplish the most simple yet difficult task: creating a community where everyone can come and be who they are? We love *our* individuality so much we cannot make room for someone else's. We are unwilling to give up even a piece of our individuality to create community where all truly feel welcome.

In some ways, I find in Unitarian Universalism the same conformity I found intolerable in my childhood faith in the Nation of Islam. The only difference is that this conformity is more dangerous for me, because this conformity asks that I make the dominant white culture my culture. From the music we sing to the styles in which we worship to the way we look at time, the dominant culture prevails. At best, we make some attempts to accommodate other cultures at certain times of the year, say Black History Month, but we do not seek to create a new culture where everyone can see their native cultures reflected with honor and dignity. People of color struggle to hold on to their identity within UU congregations. And we find that our cultures are not valued in the same way as the dominant culture.

As a black woman, I am expected to give up my individuality in order to fit in, while others hold on tightly to theirs. This conformity would try to undo all that I learned in my youth, of my inherent beauty and goodness. And that makes it a dangerous proposition for me and other people of color. I am willing to give up some parts of my individuality and culture, but not all of it. And I am increasingly unwilling to give up some if everyone else is unwilling to do the same.

True community doesn't happen unless everyone is willing to give up some of their identity as an individual to take on the identity of the group. If this doesn't happen, then we are merely a group of individuals sharing common space but not becoming a community. It doesn't mean that we go to the extremes of everyone wearing the same clothing, everyone praying the same way, if at all, or everyone believing the same things. If we were to do that, we would give up what makes us unique on the religious landscape. However, it does mean that we move individualism from the center of our focus and replace it with a new concept of shared community, in which everyone gives up a little so that we can gain a lot.

In true community we gain a lot. We gain affirmation of who we are both as individuals and as part of a group. We gain the wisdom of others who may have ideas different from our own, so that together we may create a greater vision of a future that we can work toward making real. In true community, we are supported in our life's journeys because we feel safe to be known at our deepest levels, because we are all committed to the health of the community, and it cannot be healthy unless and until its members are. And finally, we gain the commitment and the power to change the world.

Individualism is so attractive in the beginning. For many people who felt the heavy yoke of being in communities of faith where they could not fully be who they were, individualism tastes like the food they have been hungering for. But it is good only when we are starving. When we have had our fill, we look for food to sustain us for the long journey of life. That life-sustaining food can be found only in true communities of shared purpose and values, where the individual is affirmed but is not worshipped.

I sometimes think I miss the faith of my youth with its rules and its rituals. Then I realize what I miss is the power of community. One day we shall build a Unitarian Universalism in which we have the power and goodness of community, and no one gets lost in the process.

The Story We Tell

KIMBERLY WILDSZEWSKI

I grew up in rural Long Island. Polish farmers, wineries, Catholic churches, and 7-Elevens. On a sharp bend just before the start of a new hamlet sat the First Universalist Church into which I was born. A life-sized mural of an unidentified Jesus hung behind the pulpit; horsehair pews and red velvet covers adorned the sanctuary. It was as much my church—the place I learned to sit quietly, to speak from a pulpit while standing on an apple box, to hear joys and sorrows shared—as it was my playground.

I don't remember the feelings of tension or anxiety that had to have weighed on my parents and others before they left the church. I do remember, though, the following Sundays when my only remaining peer (in age and religious education) and I sat on the floor, listening, while our parents and others gathered in homes to talk about how to start a new congregation. We picked at the carpet while the adults cried, we tugged at shirt sleeves to go home while they talked finances, and we worked through our Unitarian Universalist workbooks on tolerance and Sophia Fahs and William Ellery Channing and the like to pass the time through lay sermons.

"Why did we leave?" I'd ask. Something about the minister; something about how he wouldn't be our minister anymore and how that decision was made.

In the years that followed, the small gathered body moved from homes to offices to churches to a grange hall. Over the years it had somehow become church again: we had guest ministers, consistent speakers, religious education; and before too long, the pews—this time hard wood, chipped at the edges, booming on the floor from their uneven legs—were again filled. And so, the story goes, a meeting was called to speak with UUA officials, to hire a minister, to once again let clergy bless the babies and let laypeople be fed rather than feed, to bear the fruit of a long and at times desert harvest.

And that conversation—about the association's assistance, about clergy, about authority in title and training—depleted the fellowship to fewer families than originally broke away.

More than half my life later I am now, at least by title, a representation of what wore away at the people and community I loved. I learned how to minister because of these people; I learned to love our congregational polity, to believe in the ministries of all and the significance of nurturing the small web of congregational life.

But as I came into this calling professionally, the Unitarian Universalism I experienced in my youth was spoken of not as an anomaly but as a proud fact: Unitarian Universalists are an anti-authority people.

It is, to be fair, a brilliantly empowering device. Anti-authority means we're not part of the religious mold; our theology cannot be held within a creed; we are *the uncommon denomination* of democracy in spirituality—association not denomination, gathered not formed, movement not religion. As religious America dies away and the fear of what may come out of the ashes wreaks havoc on our eldest members and leaders, we hold on to this narrative as one of our last attractive distinctions. You can be you and no one can tell you otherwise. It is this same narrative that sets up our clergy—and therefore the congregations we serve—for failure.

At a recent board of trustees retreat to discuss the systemic issues of the church I serve, with all of its blessings and challenges, we went around and around about our gratitude and frustration in seeing the same leaders hold on to the same positions for years— some for decades. We discussed territory wars—who claims what space, under whose leadership, for what purpose. Why couldn't leaders work together? Why did they speak to one another with such toxic ownership?

I admit that in my honeymoon as a new minister I happily ignored the anti-authority zeal of our congregations. My ignorance has persisted despite, at my ripe age of thirty, and with all 120 pounds of me, that as the solo minister of a congregation where I feel loved and respected, "Kiddo" and "Sweetie" are as common as "Reverend." It has persisted despite having recently heard a member, when recalling the congregation's past clergy misconduct, refer to the congregation as a people born of mistrust, despite online posts not so long ago that reminded me when moving from an assistant ministry to solo ministry that I was "becoming a real minister."

In this new place filled with new relationship and possibility, I had come to love and appreciate the matriarch and patriarch of the congregation and felt the work of co-ministering with them was worthwhile and smart. Having entrenched myself in stewardship texts and practices, I believed without hesitation that "all pledges aren't created equal" and why wouldn't I be gracious if not attentive to those who supported our budget in such substantial ways?

And then, from the corners of the retreat table, in the depths of how, why, and what to do came these words: "We just need to keep them [the respective leaders of building, grounds, and so forth] away from one another. We should create a system where they don't or can't talk to one another."

I am often kept awake at night by the things I should have said and the things I shouldn't have. If I regret anything it was my tone, but here it came—out from the visceral depths of a split congregation, from a seminary student who had no minister to remember and therefore (I learned) no clout to offer at the metaphorical cafeteria of my seminary peers, from a lifetime of defending our faith tradition from those who claim we stand on the soapbox of our Principles until right relationship is required in our own backyards—a response of fear that this new place would echo the places of old:

If we have no creed, no statement of belief, and only have this covenant thing that says our entire religion is based on a way that we promise to be with one another, and we create systems that help erode relationship, I'm not sure I care much about maintaining the building or grounds.

If the statistic is true that 88 percent of Unitarian Universalists come out of other or no faith traditions, the large majority of the work of our professional leadership (leadership who also mostly come from this 88 percent) is to teach what it means to be within this tradition. Narratives and identities, then, come out of what we teach, the stories we tell, how we hold ourselves in the positions of authority earned and given, how we hold ourselves not only in our congregations but also within our professional body.

At a recent national clergy gathering, a group of young women ministers in their twenties and thirties gathered for a meal and introductions. Many of us were meeting for the first time in person, though we greeted each other with the hugs of a finally met pen pal who knows more about our ministry and fears than some of our life partners do. Facebook has opened a world of support where we intentionally keep tabs on one another, making sure our people are thrown a lifejacket when needed.

Among conversations about theology and assistant ministries, babies and social justice, someone dared mention the soon-to-be retiring body of Unitarian Universalist clergy. Our largest generation of straight white men who, in many ways, brought us out of the heyday of humanism and into the beautiful language of spirit and holiness again; senior colleagues who grew fellowships into flagship congregations; mentors and professors and friends; retiring colleagues from whom many of us young women have benefited simply by our associations with them.

In private conversations I admitted the internal battle of wanting to stay true to my own call, spoken by the still small voice rather than the booming bearded ones, while at the same time struggling with feeling envy toward those who have moved through the search process or into leadership positions with relative ease.

If the earned authority of those in certain positions within our Ministers Association then determines the authority of others, then I fear the act of installation, in which a congregation affirms the call of a minister to lead and serve a people, is false. The installation is instead an affirmation of politics and power, and then, we hope, call.

As clergy, our sense of calling is not only toward leadership but also for love of institution and tradition. We each hold a vision for the future, but only some of us are given the authority to speak these visions into power. And so we play the game where not all pulpits or internships or mentors or geographies or size of membership are created equal.

And from our collegial gatherings we return to our congregations, to the people we serve, some of us feeling ready for engagement and lasting relationship where we are, renewed by our peer group. Others return disengaged, ready to leap on to bigger and better things—in cleaner cities, with larger staff, to congregations with power. And some of us return depleted, wondering if our ministries matter in the larger web in which we are associated; we feel a distinct divide between our call to serve for the sake of Unitarian Universalism and, instead, *serve* at best, and *put hours in* at worst, in the hopes of one day having authority.

If we have no creed, no statement of belief, and have only this covenant thing that says our entire religion is based on a way that we promise to be with one another, and we create systems that help erode relationship, I'm not sure I care much to stay associated with such a people. We must decide what we will teach, what stories we will tell, what narrative we wish to continue.

A colleague once told me, "Remember, you represent the God they don't believe in." People are hungry to be led into deeper and more trusting relationships—with themselves, others, and the world. Be careful with that hunger. Do not abuse its fragility. Do not leave them wanting because we fear breaking the narratives of mistrust into which we were born.

ON THE TRINITY OF PROMISES

In the aftermath of the changes that are coming for many Unitarian Universalist congregations, many will simply want to reassemble the old story into a meaningful and recognizable narrative, using the trinity of errors—individualism, exceptionalism, and an aversion to authority—and the precepts of the iChurch. But that story is over; it has ended. It's a story that won't take us where we must go. Living by that story means turning our backs on what we need for a bright future. This future is the Beloved Community, a community of justice, a religion and spirituality that Unitarian Universalism does have as a vital and vibrant part of our history. Unfortunately, too many of us have chosen to follow the tenets of the iChurch instead of building on the promise of covenant and Beloved Community.

To story ourselves for the future, we must restory our faith and engage the present by shaping a renewed and meaningful faith, painting with the bold strokes of promise, strokes that "[revere] the past, but [trust] the dawning future more; and [bid] the soul, in search of truth, adventure boldly and explore," as described in the hymn "As Tranquil Streams."[1] Living as twenty-first-century Unitarian Universalists means restorying a faith that is religious and

1 Lyrics by Marion Franklin Ham, "As Tranquil Streams," *Singing the Living Tradition* (Boston: Unitarian Universalist Association, 1993), hymn 145.

spiritual, covenantal and experiential, progressive and evangelical. From the trinity of promises, Beloved Community will be shaped and the future of our faith can deepen and grow again.

The essays in this section move past errors to promises—of generosity, pluralism, and imagination—which are deeply rooted in our faith traditions. This section's lead essay provides an overview of the promises and how they can shape a twenty-first-century Unitarian Universalism that embraces our theological and spiritual heritages and welcomes the future. The trinity of promises recognizes and names the cultural shifts taking place around us and gives direction for moving forward. UUA president Peter Morales deepens this theme in his essay by naming the gaps between what is and what could be. He makes an urgent and compelling appeal for a Unitarian Universalist faith shaped by significant culture change—a turning that is led by getting religion, growing leaders, and crossing borders. These, he says, will deepen our willingness to do ministry from a posture of promise.

With insight and challenge, Terasa Cooley draws on our Universalist tradition to find surprising and affirming support of the promises that are the future of our faith. Her insights and hope are examples of how the Universalist gospel of generosity and imagination can shape a bold and resilient future. Similar to Cooley's essay, Carlton Elliot Smith advocates using innovation and imagination to create and sustain meaningful religious and spiritual connections that will grow and deepen our faith in ways that some in earlier decades might never have dreamed. Bold imagination is at the heart of this essay. The historical theology and gospels of Unitarianism and Universalism still save the lives of many; he urges us to imagine with him new ways to share and sustain our message.

Some will think that military chaplaincy would be the last place to find the future promise of Unitarian Universalism, yet Captain Rebekah A. Montgomery casts aside preconceptions and names the promise of pluralism that our liberal faith brings to thousands. Her experiences, based and built on a ministry of promise, will challenge and reshape the ideas of many. And so also might the final piece in this section. Mark Stringer's essay presents the story of how one congregation and one minister wished to live the promises of generosity, pluralism, and imagination. In spite of their initial stumbling in awkwardness, they didn't let frustration or risk misdirect their urgent sense to keep moving on. This inspiring essay is a renewing call to commit to the promises of our faith.

These essays restory Unitarian Universalism with promises deep from our faith traditions. The authors proclaim the promises of generosity, pluralism, and imagination as beacons that will light the way into the next century.

The Promises of Unitarian Universalism

FREDRIC MUIR

Sociologist Robert Bellah (1927–2013) gained fame among lay readers when he chronicled "civil religion"—America's secular religion—and later when he, as lead author, explained the history, legacy, and current expressions of US public and private individualism (exceptionalism and resistance to authority) in *Habits of the Heart*.

I'd forgotten about Bellah (and sociology) until I read his obituary and subsequently ordered *The Robert Bellah Reader*. This compilation of Bellah's works rekindled my interest in the parallel development of our nation and Unitarian Universalism. Here is a subject we don't unearth enough—a topic that Unitarian minister A. Powell Davies preached in the 1940s and 50s, as did his protégé Duncan Howlett, who almost names Unitarian Universalism "the fourth American faith."

Deep in Bellah's book he provides a taste of the kind of investigation that made him so outstanding, research that makes his work relevant to what Unitarian Universalists need to discuss. He writes that a danger in American Protestant faith communities is their default posture of individualism, a posture in the making for centuries. He quotes at length the nineteenth-century Unitarian minister Henry Bellows (of All Souls Church, New York City) regarding the dangers of individualism and its impact on congregational cohesiveness. Bellah notes that this warning predicted the results of a 1995–96 survey that found one-third of Americans believe that "people have God within them, so churches aren't really necessary."[1] Though Bellah was not referencing Unitarian Universalism in particular, I wonder about his concerns and the survey results: Might American Protestantism, Unitarian Universalism, and the US story be parallel narratives—if not intermingled, then at least interdependent stories?

There are many places where one could begin to look at expressions of individualism and promising alternatives. Eboo Patel's work on pluralism is built on the limitations and exploitations revealed by Bellah and many others. Here's the way Patel, the founder of Interfaith Youth Core in Chicago, puts it in *Sacred Ground: Pluralism, Prejudice, and the Promise of America*:

> America has not been a promise to all its people. "We didn't land on Plymouth Rock," Malcolm X said. "Plymouth Rock landed on us." Whatever the faiths of the workmen who came to Mount Vernon, they laid their bricks next to Washington's slaves. We are a nation whose creed speaks of welcoming all communities and whose practice has too often crushed them. But, to borrow from Maya Angelou, the dust was determined to rise, and generous enough to carry the rest of us with. People who knew the whip of the slave master in Alabama, the business end of the police baton on the South Side of Chicago, people who could easily have called our nation a lie, chose instead to believe America was a broken promise, and gave their bodies and their blood to fix it. As Langston Hughes wrote, even though "America never was America to me," he was still committed to making the promise of this nation real, declaring one line later in his poem, "America will be."[2]

---

1   Robert N. Bellah, *The Robert Bellah Reader.* Robert N. Bellah and Stephen M. Tipton, eds., (Durham, NC: Duke University Press, 2006), 462.
2   Eboo Patel, *Sacred Ground: Pluralism, Prejudice, and the Promise of America* (Boston: Beacon Press, 2013), 16–17.

What we read in the papers and online, what we hear on the radio and television, offer common depictions and stories for both the United States and Unitarian Universalism. These two stories are strikingly similar, and the two cultures and our ideals are intertwined. Both are in for some challenging times if their future stories are not appropriately reimagined and connected with their changing subcommunities, which are broadening and deepening and creating tensions for the whole. Elemental to these challenging but promising stories is this: In the post–World War II decades—and clearly in the last twenty-five years—the United States and Unitarian Universalism have been approaching a tipping point (which will likely result in a turning point) as reflected in the changing demographics, lifestyles, and religious preferences of our nation's citizens. For example, by the year 2043 the majority of the US population will be non-white. With this historical change may come a host of other changes that may restory the American and Unitarian Universalist narratives (and many other narratives, both institutional and family). The feelings associated with this impending transition are expressed in a variety of ways: "Something isn't working here" or "This isn't the way I thought it would be." Many are confused, some are disillusioned, and out of it all may come new ideas and directions. People are struggling with and trying to shape the way we have been into the way we could be—a way shaped by exclusivity into a way that is inclusive, from an implicit monoculturalism to an explicit pluralism. Consequently, the era in which we live will be remembered as a period of transition both in the life of our nation and in Unitarian Universalism.

For several hundred years, Unitarian Universalism has been shaped by a set of qualities—the trinity of errors—that have grown to characterize us. We have deemed these our history and ignored other qualities that have shaped us. While the errors of individualism, exceptionalism, and an aversion to authority still work in some places (this may be generational), they are not going to continue to work in this century. We must look again to our heritage for a new direction, for shaping and guiding principles. Staying within our heritage is important: We are Unitarian Universalists, which means that we have a particular way of being religious and being a faith community. We subscribe to the vision of Beloved Community as imagined in our Principles.

Though he was speaking about the United States rather than Unitarian Universalism, Bill Ivey—an American folklorist and a former chair of the National Endowment for the Arts—phrases it this way: "By revisiting the nineteenth-century origins of a progressive society . . . liberals can revitalize our values. Once we *resuscitate the poetry of our roots*, filling America's value space with progressive ideas, the basic, time-tested mechanisms of government can do the rest—securing a framework of policy sturdy enough to sustain a way of life more closely aligned with real American ideals."[3] (italics mine). A trinity of promises can be rediscovered in our roots. Now is the time to resuscitate our heritage and revitalize our faith. Let us set aside the errors of our ways, speak about the poetry of promise, and build on three aspects of promise.

Generosity is at the heart of the trinity of promises. Just as individualism was the lead error from which the other two followed, generosity is the quintessential promise from which others flow and guide us in this century and into the next. Unitarian Universalism generosity is the core value in our civic and faith life. In our foundational documents, themes of generosity radiate. We are a people of a generous spirit.

Reflect on this for a moment: Can you think of a time in our nation's history, in the history of Unitarian Universalism, in your congregation, or in your relationships when progress that you felt good about was emboldened by the values of scarcity, stinginess, or fear? I cannot think of any. Every step forward, every progressive change that has occurred in our nation and faith tradition has been because of a generous spirit. Yet, as Unitarian Universalists we have missed many opportunities of promise because we have

---

3   Bill Ivey, *Handmaking America: A Back-to-Basics Pathway to a Revitalized American Democracy* (Berkeley, CA: Counterpoint, 2012), xxvi.

neglected the generosity intrinsic in our faith. When culture—and faith—are shaped by a posture of scarcity, stinginess, and fear, people are reluctant to move forward, to broaden and deepen and share what is best for all. At times like these the trinity of errors maintains control and leads in directions of little value for our future. And so we acquiesce to a shrinking and static life. Ironically, it's during such periods that we especially notice those who are living with a theology and spirit shaped by generosity. When we are around those whose spirit is generous, who give of their time, presence, and resources, we leave them feeling refreshed and whole and ready to engage another day; maybe we hope to spend more time with them or even emulate their actions and words. The same dynamics apply to our nation and to our faith. It's not too late to resuscitate "the poetry of our roots" and live into what we want to be. We can go back through our history and find those who said, "I won't be afraid. I will not live in fear. I will be of a generous spirit. I will sing songs of hope." As a people of faith, as a nation, this is our heritage, a heritage of generosity and hope.

The second promise in this trinity is pluralism. So much is going on in our nation—in the world—when it comes to pluralism, much of it under the headline of immigration. *New York Times* columnist David Brooks shared a warning to all, but most especially to conservatives: "This country is heading toward a multiethnic future. Republicans can either shape that future in a conservative direction or . . . become the receding roar of a white America that is never coming back. That's what's at stake."[4] I'm reminded of Bob Dylan, singing "The order is rapidly fadin'. And the first one now will later be last . . ." in "The Times They Are a'Changin'." The trinity of errors is the established order in Unitarian Universalism (and in the United States), but the times are a-changin'.

Pluralism can become personal very quickly. For example, my maternal and paternal families were immigrants three centuries ago. But for the others in my family it's a complex and different story. My wife is first generation American on her mother's side

---

4   David Brooks, "Pass the Bill," *New York Times*, July 12, 2013, A21.

and second generation on her dad's side. My son-in-law became a US citizen only several years ago, which means that my grandsons are first-generation Americans. You see, regardless of how or when or under what conditions your people came to the United States—regardless of the freedom and obstacles they encountered or discovered—you don't have to go back too far to learn that the challenges of pluralism are close at hand.

As Unitarian Universalists, we are a faith of immigrants. We always have been. Just like our nation, Unitarian Universalism has always welcomed others, with our flaming chalice by the door. Might we not emblazon the powerful words from "The New Colossus" on the door of every Unitarian Universalism congregation?

> Give me your tired, your poor,
> Your huddled masses yearning to breathe free;
> The wretched refuse of your teeming shore,
> Send these, the homeless, tempest-tost to me.
> I lift my lamp [our chalice] beside the golden door![5]

Those remain stirring words, and you've got to wonder: What was the committee thinking about when they chose her poetry for New York Harbor? Could you imagine—and maybe someone should—erecting a welcoming statue with Lazarus's words at the US-Mexican border? (What was good enough for New York Harbor is good enough for El Paso or Miami or LA. . . .)

The parallels between Unitarian Universalism and our nation are stunning. A strikingly high percentage of Unitarian Universalists were at one time the religious homeless and arrived on our Unitarian Universalism shores as faith immigrants. In this way, we are well versed in the value and challenges of pluralism. And, for those who grew up in the Unitarian Universalist tradition, they often leave or reconsider, and some even become "ex-pats" before returning.

---

5 Emma Lazarus, "The New Colossus," in *The Oxford Book of American Poetry*, ed. David Lehman (Oxford, England: Oxford University Press, 2006), 184.

As our nation struggles with what it means to be a nation of immigrants and with the challenges of pluralism, so Unitarian Universalism struggles with the challenges of being an immigrant faith. Pluralism is not a birthright, not something to take for granted as though it's a given, as if it's just the way it's supposed to be.

Here it's helpful to differentiate between pluralism and diversity. The United States lives with diversity, as do England, Russia, Iraq, Syria, Chile, and many other countries. Diversity simply means differences; it's a fact that wherever you find people there will be diversity. Pluralism implies diversity, but pluralism doesn't just happen. It requires hard work through engagement; we have to be intentional to create pluralism—it's an achievement. Eboo Patel says, "Pluralism is an achievement characterized by three elements: respect for different identities, positive relationships between diverse communities, and a commitment to the common good."[6]

Think how this might work in your congregation: pluralism as respect for different theologies and spiritualities; pluralism as positive relationships between the diverse communities in your church; pluralism as a commitment to the common aspirations and vision. The bridge to pluralism will not drop out of the sky or appear due to magical thinking; relationships are built by dedicated people from the ground up. We must engage each other, tell our stories to each other; we must want to meet and talk with each other. As a community of faith (and as a nation), we are diverse. Now we must build the bridge from the individualism of the iChurch to the pluralism of Beloved Community.

This is hard work, consciously choosing and working on pluralism, because it may not feel natural. People are more likely to associate with those who look, think, and behave the same as them, who share the same political, musical, and social values. If we wish to achieve pluralism, we need to go out of our way and engage with others.

Unitarian Universalist minister Mark Morrison-Reed has documented our faith's history of addressing many of these issues. He

6 Eboo Patel, "From Diversity to Pluralism," *Sojourners*, June 2013, 14.

notes something about our version of pluralism that we are often reluctant to name, but must be addressed. According to Morrison-Reed, the terms *pluralism* and *diversity* are really "UU code for 'persons of color and Latino/Latina/Hispanic people.' Why do we say diversity [and pluralism]? It saves time. If we had to list everyone—Asians and South Asians, Native Americans and Inuits, Filipinos and Pacific Islanders, Latino/Latina/Hispanic peoples and, of course, members of the African diaspora, and whomever else I have missed—we would not finish the sentence until tomorrow."[7]

In just a couple of decades, non-Anglos will comprise the majority of Americans. Anglos, who have comprised the vast majority of Unitarian Universalists for centuries, will become a smaller and smaller pool of possible members while non-Anglos grow steadily and become the future of our faith. With this dramatic demographic shift will come frame-bending changes in UU congregations.

We are faith immigrants who have found each other and our home, called Unitarian Universalism. But in sharing our aspirations and commitments, who have we left out, who has been marginalized, who are the other faith immigrants who might want in but don't feel welcome? Pluralism means learning how to make space for all the immigrants who want to arrive at our shores, who yearn to breathe free.

The last promise in this trinity is imagination. Novelist and essayist Marilynne Robinson writes, "I am convinced that the broadest possible exercise of imagination is the thing most conducive to human health, individual and global."[8] If we as a community of faith or as a nation stumble, fall, lose our balance, or break, it will in part be due to our unwillingness to be imaginative, to bring bold creative reflection to the issues and challenges we face. Imagination means seeing and thinking beyond the present,

---

7   Mark Morrison-Reed, *Darkening the Doorways: Black Trailblazers and Missed Opportunities in Unitarian Universalism* (Boston: Skinner House Books, 2011), 302.

8   Marilynne Robinson, "Imagination and Community" in *When I Was a Child I Read Books* (New York: Farrar, Straus & Giroux, 2012), 26.

it means being a faith where "We would be one in living for each other to show to all a new community."[9]

To trust the dawning future requires imagination. Peter Buffett (one of the children of financial guru Warren Buffett), in a July 26, 2013, op-ed essay published in the *New York Times*, spoke of the frame-bending changes that must be initiated by charitable organizations. He concludes with these words: "What we have is a crisis of imagination. Albert Einstein said that you cannot solve a problem with the same mind-set that created it."

Bold imagination brought Unitarian Universalism to a remarkable and transformational place. The 1967 UUA "Report of the Committee on Goals" found that 47 percent of Unitarian Universalists agreed that being a woman would hamper one's effectiveness as a minister. Morrison-Reed reflects on this and asks, "What happened in the ensuing years? The number of women grew from about 21 in 1968 to 199 in 1987, and in 2010, women make up over half of our active ministry. Might hamper her effectiveness? Apparently not."[10] In short, a significant change in mindset occurred. This is also reflected in another significant change: A 1989 UUA Commission on Appraisal survey reported that 66 percent of Unitarian Universalists made a similarly pessimistic prediction about openly lesbian, gay, or bisexual ministers. Today, the Unitarian Universalist Association includes more than seventy LGBTQ ministers.[11] We have witnessed how imagination can change us. Yet, we still have changes to initiate and complete. For example, while the success of welcoming and ordaining women and LGBTQ folks is a story we can be proud of, Morrison-Reed wonders what happened to African-American ministers in the UUA during this explosion of imaginative, historical, and prophetic leadership. Put simply: not much.

---

9 Samuel Anthony Wright, "We Would Be One," *Singing the Living Tradition* (Boston: Unitarian Universalist Association, 1993), hymn 318.
10 Morrison-Reed, 300.
11 Ibid., 300–301.

Individualism, exceptionalism, and our aversion to authority did not create the transformational opportunities that have taken place. Generosity, pluralism, and imagination did, and they are the way forward. The trinity of promises must shape the story we tell about ourselves; the promises are an opportunity to restory Unitarian Universalism.

The narrative we tell, the story we rehearse, is critical to who we become. Robert Bellah notes, "Narrative . . . is the way we understand our lives. . . . Narrative is not only the way we understand our personal and collective identities, it is the source of our ethics, our politics, and our religion."[12]

Jacqueline Lewis, minister at Middle Collegiate Church in New York City, says that "our identities are formed by stories told to us, about us, and around us. We are living texts, formed by multiple, interweaving, competing, and, sometimes, conflicting stories that we receive from our culture via our parents, other adults, our peers, the media, and congregational life."[13] She names the challenge that so many Unitarian Universalism congregations wish they could address: "People and congregations are formed by stories; leadership can create and sustain multi-racial and multicultural congregations" in spite of the counterstories that undermine the building of Beloved Community. The trinity of errors is our counterstory; we must restory Unitarian Universalism.

We have so much to do, and yet we are so close, because so much has been done. In her memoir, US Supreme Court justice Sonia Sotomayor writes, "Sometimes, no matter how long we've carried a dream or prepared its way, we meet the prospect of its fulfillment with disbelief, startled to see it in daylight. In part that may be because, refusing to tempt fate, we have never actually allowed ourselves to expect it."[14]

---

12 Bellah, 10.
13 Jacqueline J. Lewis, *The Power of Stories: A Guide for Leading in Multi-Racial and Multi-Cultural Congregations* (Nashville: Abingdon Press, 2008), 5.
14 Sonia Sotomayor, *My Beloved World* (New York: Alfred A. Knopf, 2013), 286.

Is that you too? Is that us? Our faith community? Is it our nation? It feels like we are so close to what we aspire to be; yet we are still so far from where we want to be. So we keep coming back to the promises of generosity, pluralism, and imagination, over and over again. Thank goodness! Because Beloved Community is who we could be. It's who we want to be. We see glimpses of this new reality breaking through, moments of what it could be to live in the promises.

Drawing on the rhythms of generosity, pluralism, and imagination, we will shape and tell our story—who we have been and the opportunities we have missed. But let's not spend too much precious time on the past. Let's also tell the story of who we will be; let's share the poetry of our roots.

Our Historic Opportunity

PETER MORALES

The world does not have to be this way.

This, I believe, is the fundamental conviction shared among Unitarian Universalists. Life does not have to be filled with conflict, hatred, violence, greed, loneliness, mindless consumption, and injustice. This has been a core conviction of our religious tradition throughout our history. Our modern movement was born in opposition to religious perspectives that argued that human beings are inherently evil (Calvinism and most of Protestantism) and that we need to accept our fate (medieval Catholicism). We replaced pessimism and resignation with optimism and activism. We replaced a vision of sinners in the hand of an angry God with a vision of a loving God who accepts everyone.

Our conviction that life can be transformed is based on both experience and vision. We have seen glimpses of the promised land. Each of us has experienced love, generosity, and unspeakable beauty. We have experienced the grace of unearned blessings. And we share a vision of human possibility in Beloved Community that gives us hope.

We have never had more reason to believe that life does not have to be this way than today. Never before in human history have we had the means to secure a decent, dignified life for all people. And never before has there been the potential to move beyond the narrow tribalisms of race, ethnicity, culture, and social class. These tribalisms rationalize oppression and breed violence.

Another core conviction shared among Unitarian Universalists is that we can and should play a far larger role in transforming human lives than we presently do. I have always felt this way—ever since attending my first UU service twenty years ago. I have always been puzzled and frustrated that we are such a small movement. This isn't about growth for the sake of growth, it is about making a difference. For me, trying to grow our faith is a moral imperative on the level of feeding the hungry and sheltering the homeless.

So here is the challenge as I see it. At the personal level, people need religious community. We are relational creatures who only become fully human in a web of loving and committed relationships. This is the ideal of covenanted community. At the global level, the world desperately needs movements that embrace human diversity, are committed to compassion and justice, and that seek to live in harmony with the web of life on earth.

The gap between what we are as Unitarian Universalists and what is needed is huge. We remain small while the need is enormous. And another thing is true: We have enormous potential.

What We Need—and Don't Need

Many or perhaps all of us have suffered through listening to a musical performance in which all the notes were played perfectly but the performance was lifeless and cold. The same can be true of a theatrical performance: An actor can deliver all the lines perfectly and not create a convincing character. The flip side is also true. I have heard music performed where a few notes were missed but the music came through powerfully. I have witnessed theater in which a few lines were inaudible or unintelligible, but the play came alive and moved my soul. The notes are not the music; the words are not the play.

As a religious movement, we have been too focused on hitting the notes rather than playing the music.

In visiting scores of our congregations over the years, I have seen two distinctly different outcomes in congregations that do virtually the same things when welcoming visitors. They may have the same checklist: a welcome table front and center, introduction of visitors, follow up, and so forth, and yet the feeling in one congregation can be completely different from another. In one place the congregation plays the music of religious hospitality; in the other, the congregation hits the notes but makes little music.

We have indulged in an idolatry of technique (and I include myself among the "sinners" in this regard). We have thought that we would grow if we simply did governance right, or did religious education better, or had better music, or preached better, or did better marketing, or embraced the language of reverence, or used social media better, or used Spanish language hymns and readings, or were more spiritual, or heaven knows what. But the checklists are never enough; they are just the notes, not the music.

Culture Change: Get Religion, Grow Leaders, Cross Borders

In order to focus on the music, we do not need technical fixes. We need culture change. Pockets of this culture change are emerging all over our movement, and it fills me with hope. But they are not nearly enough. Our times demand more. In an era in which people are leaving organized religion by the millions, we need to do much better at creating congregations and communities that touch people's souls and help them participate in ways that engage their highest ideals and their passion to make a difference. Generosity, pluralism, and imagination promise a way forward.

A true generosity of spirit is eager to share—and that means Unitarian Universalists sharing ourselves and our communities as well as our treasure. A religious movement that "gets religion" reaches out to others not to proselytize but to engage and welcome them. The phrase *get religion* usually speaks to a powerful conversion experience and a determination to mend one's ways. Using it in our context generates mild shock among many Unitarian Universalists because we don't use that kind of language. But perhaps we should. We need to take ourselves seriously as a religious movement.

We have been so wary for so long of being like evangelical fundamentalists that we often lose sight of the fact that we too are a religious movement. Religion is not and never has been about agreeing to a set of theological or philosophical propositions. Religion has always been about so much more. At its center is a community of people who come together to carry on a tradition and to shape a common future—what some call a community of memory and hope.

If we want people to join with us to build spiritual communities and to build a compassionate and sustainable world, we have to be passionate. Signs that this is happening among us include the best worship services taking place at General Assembly, in so many of our congregations, and among our young. Consider the bravery and determination we show when a sea of yellow "Standing on the Side of Love" T-shirts show up in the struggle for marriage equality, economic justice, environmental justice, immigration, and more.

For me, religion is not about *having* faith but about being faithful. Faith is not something you or I possess. It is a relationship; really, a set of ongoing relationships. My religion is about being faithful to what I hold most dear, about being faithful to my commitments to people close to me, about being faithful to what I hold sacred.

When I think about imagination as a promising way to restore Unitarian Universalism, I think about our commitment to affirm and promote a movement that is democratic and anti-authority. We value freedom. No, actually, we cherish freedom. We believe in democratic process. We believe all voices have a right to be heard. Mostly, that is a good thing. Mostly.

But it has a shadow side, too. There is a sting of truth to the old joke that given a choice between going to heaven and going to a discussion about heaven, Unitarian Universalists would choose the discussion. Sometimes I fear we have crossed the line from making our congregational polity a means toward a larger end and have made polity and democratic process an object of worship.

The unspoken truth is that what appear to be our most democratic processes—our congregational meetings and our annual General Assembly—are clearly not democratic and often lack imagination. Take the typical congregational meeting as an example. Often it is a struggle to get a quorum of, say, 15 percent of the members. And those who do show up are far from representative. They typically skew heavily to older members and those who enjoy public debate. Younger people and parents with younger children are usually underrepresented. At General Assembly the delegates are largely self-selected; they are simply the people who have the interest, time, and the means to attend. We devote enormous time, energy, and expense to rituals of democracy that may or may not actually do the will of the people.

We idolize polity and process. Some Unitarian Universalists believe that if we somehow get governance right everything else will follow. But an organization with democratic process can be healthy or unhealthy, thriving or in decline, effective or bumbling. The sad truth is that Unitarian Universalists often process things to death. We confound passing a resolution with actually doing something. We disempower everyone and call it democracy.

Effective and imaginative organizations know how to grow leaders. They know how to identify potential leaders, nurture them, empower them, and, yes, hold them accountable. Healthy congregations and movements know how to build trust. If I can trust you to do something well, you are free to use your gifts and I am freed to use mine. A profound spiritual and relational dimension is at work here. Trust begins as a gift, but ultimately it is earned over time.

In times as volatile as ours, we need leaders. We need leaders who are visionary, competent, credible, and inspirational. That does not mean we need narcissistic prima donnas or petty tyrants. Good leaders help others be their best selves. Good leaders care deeply about the people they lead. Good leaders are humble.

In our movement we need ministers who see themselves as religious leaders. However, healthy organizations know how to share leadership, how to let different people lead at different times. Leadership for our next generation cannot be exclusively or primarily ministerial.

Ultimately, this is about community. We are at our best when we learn both how to lead and how to follow and when to lead and when to follow. At our best we identify each other's gifts and encourage each other to use them. We empower one another by placing trust in one another. We authorize one another to act on behalf of the greater good. And we hold each other accountable without paralyzing one another.

Think about the people you know in Unitarian Universalism. Imagine what we might do, what we might become, if we truly learned to grow leaders.

Pluralism is another promise that will shape our UU future story. Pluralism is a challenge for us—it suggests change. Consider the times in your life when you were profoundly changed, when your view of yourself and your life was fundamentally altered, turning points that you would call religious experiences. If you are like me, these times were powerful experiences that involved your senses and emotions, not just your intellect. For many of us, these moments took place during childhood, adolescence, or young adulthood. Granted, intellectual insights are important, but what really formed me were a handful of experiences.

There is a powerful lesson here for us as a religious movement. Unitarian Universalists tend to be better at the intellectual and cognitive part of religion than the emotional and experiential part.

Some years ago my congregation sent a delegation to Guatemala, led by Charlie Clements, the president of the Unitarian Universalist Service Committee at the time. I was one of ten people who went on that trip, and we were interested in human rights work and seeing that work firsthand. The experience of seeing a refugee camp full of survivors of horrific massacres, seeing mass graves, meeting indigenous leaders, encountering women and children, and seeing and smelling the poverty had a dramatic effect. A hundred workshops, even complete with photos, would have had little impact. However, the experience of being in Guatemala and meeting these oppressed people face to face turned the members of the delegation into human-rights activists for life. We organized a partnership that has resulted in a scholarship program, aimed mostly at girls, that now has more than fifty students and has raised more than one hundred thousand dollars. That partnership is changing lives—both those of the Mayan youngsters and of the Unitarian Universalists who are involved in this work. It all began with direct experience.

When we expose ourselves and our fellow Unitarian Universalists to experiences outside our usual comfort zones, we cross borders. We do it for ourselves personally, we do it for the people we encounter, we do it for our congregations. Crossing borders cannot be patronizing and condescending, something we do *for* "them." Rather, it breaks out of the invisible prisons created by class, culture, race, ethnicity. Like most groups, we Unitarian Universalists have unintentionally created a culture that confines us.

Our values and principles—compassion, spiritual depth, acceptance of knowledge and wisdom from many sources, peace, justice, sustainability—are values that are fundamentally human. They span cultures. They embrace pluralism. However, our institutional expression of these pluralistic values continues to look (and feel) very Anglo, very Protestant, very Yankee, very educated middle class. If we are to break out of this prison, we must cross borders of class, culture, and race; we must embrace pluralism.

An Exciting Future

I see amazing and exciting movement in our faith regarding fully embracing human diversity. Our work to oppose racism, our increasingly diverse ministry, the nurturing of multicultural worship styles, our inclusion of music from many cultures and ages, and the new Unitarian Universalist College of Social Justice are all healthy and hopeful developments. We just need to do a lot more, and soon.

Imagine a Unitarian Universalism in which our youth, our young adults, our ministers in formation, and, yes, all of us have the experience of connecting with people outside our usual circle. That experience would unleash a quantum leap of spiritual growth and passion to change the world.

Imagine being born a thousand years ago. You were likely to die young. Your chances of living to age sixty or seventy were slight. You would experience the painful deaths of siblings and friends. You would be illiterate. You would never see distant lands. The image of a Beloved Community had to be located in the next life, for the possibility of a decent life for everyone in this life was zero. The chance of controlling disease and famine was slim to none. A thousand years ago you and your neighbors were not virtually powerless; you were truly powerless.

For the first time in human history people have the power to create the world our ancestors have dreamed of for millennia. We have always been able to love our children. Today we still can love them, but we can also feed them, educate them, and heal them when they are ill. We can nurture their talents and open them to endless possibilities.

As I write this I can check the news and see that there is war in the Middle East, that economic inequality runs rampant, that millions still live in fear because they are gay, that women are still oppressed, that environmental destruction is rampant, that fundamentalists impose their rigid tyrannies, and so forth, ad nauseum.

And it doesn't have to be like this. And we can make a difference. Yes, we are tiny. We can't remake the world by ourselves. But when we reach out in love, when we join forces among ourselves and with others, we have untold and untapped power for good. We can create loving communities in our congregations and use them as base stations for extending love, justice, and peace into the wider world.

This is religious work, the work of engaged spirituality. This is about connecting with our selves, our tradition, our spiritual communities, and our wider world.

Saying that we have a historic opportunity sounds trite, like some tedious graduation speech. We have heard the phrase so often we are immune. What words can I possibly use? Maybe I should say we have *the* historic opportunity.

Fear holds us back. We are afraid of failure, afraid of looking silly. We are afraid—no, that is too mild—we are paranoid about losing our individual independence. At some deep level we are afraid of succeeding. We are afraid of the responsibility that comes with owning our power.

We need not fear. We must not let our fears hold us back.

We have promises built on and shaped by generosity, imagination, and pluralism, promises that will change our lives and the world.

The Global Challenge of Universalism

TERASA G. COOLEY

I am not one who usually indulges in romanticizing Universalism. While I agree with many others that we could have benefited more as a faith by following the Universalist paths, I worry that if we look through the rosy glow of romance at our Universalist past, we may not clearly see the hard challenges it presented then, and still does now.

And yet I am willing to risk criticism by applying the challenge of Universalism to our current cultural context and see what it might say about the promise of our future.

In my role as program and strategy officer at the Unitarian Universalist Association, I am charged with overseeing all program areas as well as key strategic initiatives, such as Congregations and Beyond[1] and recent moves toward rebranding. Within the program team I assembled, the International Office is now included, while it used to lodge on its own in the President's Office. The confluence of working on the paradigm-shifting concepts in Congregations and Beyond and immersing myself more in UUA international work and relationships has brought me to a distinctly uncomfortable awareness of how poorly we have been realizing our Universalist promise.

---

1 For a deeper explanation of Congregations and Beyond see the webpage "Vision for Unitarian Universalism: Congregations and Beyond," www.uua.org/vision/beyond/index.shtml.

A paper delivered by Peter Morales in 2012 was the impetus for what came to be called Congregations and Beyond, the UUA effort to deeply examine current culture shifts in the religious landscape and ask how we might need to shift our structures and efforts to be more responsive and relevant to these changes. The dramatic decrease in Americans' attachment to religious institutions, especially younger Americans, demands that we ask whether we need to change our assumptions about what religious community can or should be.

I am one of those people who used to adamantly declare, "You can't be a real Unitarian Universalist without being a member of a congregation!" The belief behind this assertion is that one's faith is best lived out in a community that supports, challenges, and deepens one's faith. I still believe that. But I have come to also see the ways in which this kind of declaration assumes a model of congregational life not accessible to a variety of peoples and life circumstances, and narrows our vision to include only those who wish to join us in the particular style and cultural expression of our existing congregations.

What about those who don't live near one of our congregations? What about those who feel alienated by the dominant culture we unconsciously express? What about those who may not be stirred by our style of worship? What notion of hospitality is it that allows us to righteously point a finger and declare, "You're not one of us!" Is it really just about us? These kinds of questions came to me as I delved more deeply into the paradigm shifts required of us by the Congregations and Beyond analysis.

I am a lifelong Unitarian Universalist. I have been ordained for more than twenty-five years and have served our faith both in congregations and in UU institutions. I love our faith, believe in our saving message, and devote myself to its furtherance. And it feels like I'm only now beginning to see the depth of the ways in which we limit ourselves, and thereby our faith's potential, through the limited lenses we apply.

The second jolt in this awareness came when I started to work more closely with our International Office. In January 2014 I attended the conference of the International Council of Unitarians and Universalists, which included participants from twenty-five countries.

I will admit that I used to be one of those UUs who never really understood why some people were so engaged with our international partners. It's not that I didn't think the rest of the world was important (I hope!) but more that I had the typical UU aversion to anything that seemed remotely to resemble "missionary" work or (worse) charity to those less fortunate. If I had looked even deeper, I would have found a subconscious awareness and fear of my own intercultural incompetence. As I walked into this conference I found I was quite nervous about how to even talk to someone from an extremely different culture. The fact that I had some fairly deep friendships with people from different cultures didn't pierce my insecurity.

The incredible openness and eagerness that I encountered with our international partners quickly broke through this discomfort, and I began to view my previous attitudes with regret and some shame. In the course of a few short days, I had some profound conversations that showed me that, rather than feeling like something was being asked of me that I wasn't sure I could give, something of great value was being offered to me that deepened my faith. I encountered people for whom our faith was a lifeline and who in return placed their lives on the line for our faith.

One conversation in particular stands out for me. I was talking with Rev. Tet Gallardo, a newly ordained minister from the Philippines, and Rev. Fulgence Ndagijimana, the founder of the Unitarian Church of Bujumbura, Burundi. We were discussing what it was that might cause people, even children, to commit violent acts of atrocity. Tet's answer was immediate: dislocation. Fulgence agreed and expanded: There is no place on earth anymore where people do not feel the effects of being alienated from native culture, lands, family, access to basic human rights. In his land of Burundi, he saw all too clearly the pull charismatic and cruel leaders could exert on those feeling so unmoored. And what other message is out there to counter such pressure? The answer was clear to him: The values of Unitarian Universalism offer a new and essential path. For we acknowledge that there are no easy answers and yet still offer a clear choice: choose love and life. He felt that if he did not offer our message to Bujumbura he would be turning his back on his people.

I became an overnight convert to the importance of our international work and relationships, seeing not only that our faith has some essential importance in the broader world but, even more important, what this model of faithful living can offer to Unitarian Universalism. I began to dig deeper into our oft-made assumption that Unitarian Universalism is primarily a North American phenomenon. Many others share my distrust of anything that smacks of assuming that what is good for Americans should or could be good for anyone else. I'm also aware that many of our international partners have been put off by a certain kind of unintentional American imperialism that the Unitarian Universalist Association has exhibited. And I know that in previous times the UUA lacked the resources to actively invest in helping to establish groups beyond our borders. But I now wonder whether our hesitancy does not also have the same root as my insecurity in January. We have not always been stellar at displaying our intercultural competence. Navigating American cultural divisions has proven to be hard enough; crossing international boundaries may seem like a bridge too far.

With new online technologies, we can now offer more resources and structural support to international groups than ever before. Developing relationships with people separated by continents has never been easier. But it is clear to me that simply using technology in more sophisticated ways will not immediately make us more internationally accessible or oriented. We need theology as well.

At the 2014 General Assembly, I was asked to deliver the John Murray Distinguished Lecture. This is a workshop sponsored by the Murray Grove Association to advance the history and values of Universalism. When preparing for this lecture, I thought I would simply add a theological gloss to my typical introduction to the concepts of Congregations and Beyond. Universalism in particular should offer credence to our desire to move farther out into the highways and byways, even the information superhighways, to bring our values into the world.

But as I reimmersed myself in Universalist history and theology, something I hadn't done for quite some time, I found myself increasingly struck by the parallels between the cultural context of Universalism at the time of its founding and the culture shifts happening today. These parallels left me feeling that our Universalist forebears were reaching out from the past to shove us toward taking up the Universalist challenge once again.

Here are some parallels I saw:

- Early Universalist times were filled with great societal divisions and upheavals. We need only look at the current maps of red and blue states to see the similarity.

- Early Universalists were often affected by a greater awareness of the diversity of the world and experienced both culture clashes and increased contact with people different from themselves. Today, no one can doubt the impact of globalization—both its challenges and its opportunities.

- Early Universalists were stimulated to transformations in theology by larger paradigmatic changes in the ways people viewed human agency—fueled by a technology, namely book publishing. Today the paradigm shift in human experience brought about by the Internet and social media is only beginning to become clear to us.

Universalist theology offered a compelling response to these culture shifts changing the ground underneath early American beginnings. It was so compelling that both men and women were stirred to leave their homes and suffer numerous indignities to offer this saving message to as many others as possible.

The following definition of Universalist theology, distilled by my colleague Stefan Jonasson, surely offers a compelling answer to the challenges of our own times and to the problems of early times:

- Whatever else God may be or not be, God is love——and even if we reject belief in God at all, we can still believe in the power of love

- No individual or tradition possesses the whole truth, but each grasps a piece of what is true, perhaps several such pieces

- All people are somehow sacred, whether we call this an inner divinity or simply human dignity

- The same fate—whatever it may be—awaits us all

And so, why are we so reluctant to share this theology? Is it not the answer to dislocation that Rev. Fulgence believes has so much power for his people? Is it not the thread of connection people so badly need in our disconnected lives?

I have become convinced that a religious response must balance itself between two true and seemingly opposing polarities. Human beings need to feel honored and seen in their uniqueness —to be able to develop and grow in ways that are uniquely theirs. At the same time, we need to acknowledge that alone we are not sufficient—we need others to challenge and support us and we need to give to others as well. Tipped too far in one of these directions and we become tyrants of our individualism; too far toward the other, we stifle the incredible spectrum of human expression in favor of communal conformity. At its best, Unitarian Universalism has the unique ability to offer a balance beam between these two needs.

The promise of Unitarian Universalism, the fullest expression of Universalist theology and Unitarian reason, can be realized only if we cast off certain assumptions, either conscious or subconscious, about what embodies and defines us. The clarion call I hear from our Universalist ancestors begs me to challenge the assumption that ours is only a North American faith and to experiment boldly in creating multiple kinds of communities and expressions of religious life. I have been seeing signs of our willingness to move in these directions, but I believe we need more than signs and intentions; we need actual attitudinal and behavioral shifts if we are to heed this call.

Taking up this challenge requires us to be evangelists once more. But evangelism in the twenty-first century requires different skills than those of the nineteenth. (Readers may be relieved to know that knocking on doors is not required!) I could detail a toolkit, but new technical means are not all that's required. Certain culture shifts are called for. Three in particular include developing intercultural competence, signaling clear identity, and moving from brokenness to resilience.

Developing Intercultural Competence

Intercultural competence is a concept that Unitarian Universalists have been learning only recently. At its most basic, it points us toward an ability to effectively and respectfully interact with those whose cultures or languages, or both, differ from our own. This is not an "all people are the same" assumption. It asks us to delve deeply into our own cultural assumptions and experiences, to celebrate and challenge them, as well as to listen deeply and understand the culturally specific values and norms that others bring.

Universalism was also well ahead of its time in this regard. From eighteenth-century Universalist evangelist George de Benneville:

> The spirit of Love will be intensified to Godly proportions when reciprocal love exists between the entire human race and each of its individual members. That love must be based upon mutual respect for the differences in color, language, and worship, even as we appreciate and accept with gratitude the differences that tend to unite the male

and female of all species. We do not find those differences obstacles to love.[2]

While many of us would intellectually agree with de Benneville's statement, we have been challenged in figuring out what this would actually look like as a lived practice. Some of our congregations have moved toward some diversity in worship—in my home congregation in Brookline, Massachusetts, we regularly sing out of the Spanish language hymnal, even while acknowledging some discomfort. But few venture too far or too often from the typical Protestant order of worship with fairly traditional Western classical music.

In 2010 producer Ridley Scott invited people from all over the globe to videotape some portion of their day, only on July 24, 2010, with the intent of addressing these topics: Tell us your story. Tell us what you fear. Show us what is in your pockets. Scott and his team put out this request on social media not knowing who might respond. The global community responded. From Australia to Zambia, eighty thousand people uploaded their video stories, totaling over forty-five hundred hours of documentation of life on this earth. One can imagine the enormity of the task of editing this material down to a feature length movie, but the result was worth it: one hour and thirty-five minutes of pure magic.[3] Watching just the trailer for it makes me cry, so stirring is its evocation of the diversity and challenge and beauty of life all over the world.

If we were to have the resources to do a similar video showing all the ways in which Unitarian Universalists worship all over the world, I think we would be amazed at the evidence of diversity that most of us in North America are hardly aware of. And, I believe, we would become aware of how enriched our lives would be if we were more in relationship with one another.

Border crossing is a concept Unitarian Universalists have recently been exploring—the 2012 General Assembly, which

---

2 Albert D. Bell, *The Life and Times of Dr. George de Benneville* (Universalist Church of America, 1953), 65.
3 Watch the "Life in a Day" video at www.youtube.com/user/lifeinaday.

focused on justice, gave many of us a firsthand view of the injustices of our immigration system. Through new structures like the Unitarian Universalist College of Social Justice, more of us are going on trips literally across borders. Many UU congregations have partner church relationships with communities in other countries. The renewed energy in these directions is impressive. The spiritual practice will be how these opportunities truly transform us and our communities and not just serve as justice tourism.

Signaling Clear Identity

The other day a colleague of mine and I pulled into a parking lot and saw a Prius with several bumper stickers: Coexist, Reelect Barack Obama, Love the Earth. Immediately we both said in unison, "Must be a Unitarian Universalist." This is a stereotype of course, but for a reason: Unitarian Universalism has an identity in the broader world. Through everything we do and say and embody, we send a signal about what Unitarian Universalism is. In some cases the identity that comes across is good. At a recent conference on social entrepreneurship for nonprofits, I met numerous people who work for social justice or community organizations, and almost every one of them said, "I know Unitarian Universalists. You're the ones who show up!" And we do have that reputation.

We also have a variety of other reputations that are not so good or are confusing to outsiders. The Garrison Keillor jokes at our expense are funny, or not so funny, for a reason. ("What is a Unitarian Universalist? Unitarian means one, and Universalist means everything, so a UU is someone who believes in one of everything.") It used to be that Unitarian Universalists were prominent in public offices. Now Barack Obama has to cover over his UU past.

We have struggled forever with how to convey who we are, what we do, and why we matter. Some of this struggle is theological (even the early Universalists had ongoing battles and schisms over theology). Some of this struggle is political—how do we take public stands on issues without risking too much division and alienation? Some of it is cultural—we often don't like to talk about ourselves or our beliefs out of fear that it will be too "evangelical." Part of it is just that we tend to use too darned many words!

In the cacophony of words and messages and memes and tweets and Facebook posts, the core values of Unitarian Universalism can easily get tuned out. Finding compelling ways to tell our story and share our values does not just require the correct theological words. It also requires us to speak of our experience, to tell a story, to use images more than words.

In applying these principles to our work at the Unitarian Universalist Association, we've been astonished to realize how much of our communication assumes that our only audience is those who are already UUs. It's not that our internal constituencies are unimportant, but if we can't figure out how to develop an outward-facing identity, how can we expect congregations to do so? We are still working on what all this means for us at the UUA. It's like developing new muscles. Finding core messaging and signaling clear identity is our ongoing work.

But again, these are largely techniques and technologies. What of the larger culture shift required? It begins with this core concept: It's not all about *us*! The initial Facebook furor over the release of our new logo had certain common themes, one of them being "I don't like it." And I certainly understand that Unitarian Universalists need to feel that they can see themselves in our public images. But what if, ultimately, it's not about you? How do we develop the ability to see through an outsider's eyes, to contemplate what others may need of us, rather than primarily what we may need? One branding consultant we interviewed early in our process described it this way: The job of an organization is to tell a hero's story (think Joseph Campbell) in such a way that the story is not about the institution. It's about whether the hearer can recognize their own story within the larger one.

The thing is, in the absence of our voice and story in the public square, others fill the gap. One only need look at a recent holiday advertisement put together by Apple. It features a family gathering and a teenager who seems completely absorbed by his iPhone rather than participating in the family activities. In fact what he is doing is filming the family, and then he shares his video with great love. Apple is telling a story of love and connection—in essence, spiritual values—to sell its products. Can we too promote spiritual values in service of something larger?

Moving from Brokenness to Resilience

I often hear converts to Unitarian Universalism tell this story: I left the religion of my past because it constantly talked about how we were sinful, degraded people. I want to hear a message of wholeness and belief in the basic goodness of humanity. A lot of us can hear ourselves in this story. But what this often fails to convey is the recognition that we are essentially, by virtue of our existence in this world, broken by the challenges of life and often feel isolated or alienated from others and our core values.

When I was in the parish it broke my heart to hear people come to me with some version of this story: "I'm going through a divorce and I can't tell my fellow congregants because I don't feel like I can talk openly about my sense of shame. Why don't we talk about how we all make mistakes and need forgiveness?"

If our religious tradition fails to acknowledge woundedness and pain, we leave an essential gap in spiritual development. Ironically, it leaves people stuck in their pain and fails to help people develop something we all need: resilience. Someone in a congregation once said to me, "I will start focusing on helping other people once I've done my own healing." When does anyone ever feel completely healed?

Finding a way to acknowledge pain and pointing people to a way out of it requires a fine balance. Conservative religions and groups acknowledge pain and point a finger at others as the cause. They essentially leave a person broken but feeling patched together with the glue of bitterness and resentment. Even attempts to pull people together in the midst of pain acts out a story of imperialism. Take the Super Bowl commercial aired in 2012 featuring Clint Eastwood ("It's Halftime in America") talking about how we all have to come together as Americans to show the rest of the world how superior we are!

In response to this kind of message, three new UU ministers, Erik Resly, Robin Bennett, and Jonathan Rogers, produced a video called "Wholetime in America" that challenges this premise. In it they say,

> This isn't about the superiority of our country. It's about the strength of our souls. . . . My faith is a faith for the whole. It tells the story of a shared human journey. . . . In a culture obsessed with domination, I as a UU will continue to share a different gospel, the story of cooperation, of people coming together to find that sacredness within each of us, and to live the salvation available to all. [4]

This is, of course, essentially a Universalist gospel, one that helps people see themselves and their brokenness in a larger context in which they can feel held and healed and inspired to offer that healing to others. This can happen within congregations, yes. But it doesn't require a congregation to communicate this message and inspire this kind of resilience and faith. If we are offering this only to those who have already found us in physical buildings, we leave the larger world abandoned to countermessages of division and increased alienation.

We demonstrate this spirit through our social justice work in the world. And more is needed. At the 2014 General Assembly in Providence, Rhode Island, for the first time we went out into the community to proclaim our message of love through our sponsorship of the art installation WaterFire and our willingness to encounter others with the story of our faith. It was truly transformational.

---

4 Watch the video "Wholetime in America" at www.youtube.com/watch?v=Y-IhZocknKuM.

Can we take up the Universalist challenge once again? Can we look outside our well-worn notions of who "we" are? Can we listen as well as speak? Can we offer our values to a world in desperate need of wholeness? Can we be open to the healing that comes from others?

I am often asked whether I see a real future for Unitarian Universalism. I do. But it will look and feel different than it does today. It does not require us to abandon who we have been and what we do but to expand into a fuller expression of the values we have been given by our spiritual ancestors. Love is hard. Do it anyway.

Reimagining Unitarian Universalism

CARLTON ELLIOTT SMITH

The ability to imagine landed me on the doorstep of liberal religion in the mid-1990s. At the end of a one-year fellowship as a staff writer for Religion News Service, I stood at a crossroads. One path led to the possibility of a career in religious journalism; the other, to a career in parish ministry within a denomination I was only beginning to know—the Unitarian Universalist Association.

I had graduated from Howard University School of Divinity two years prior, where one of my classmates was Alma Crawford, a minister already serving a small intentionally diverse start-up Unitarian Universalist congregation in Washington, DC. When I left the Pentecostal church where I had experienced my sense of call into the ministry in my final year of study, it was Alma and Professor Elias Farajajé-Jones (now Ibrahim Farajajé of Starr King School for the Ministry) who encouraged me to consider Unitarian Universalist ministry.

The prospect had a natural appeal to me. Having been raised in a black United Methodist church in the Deep South, my religious upbringing had none of the hellfire and damnation that my Pentecostal cousins and childhood friends had been taught. The church I grew up in founded a school for freed African Americans in 1866 that became Rust College—the place where my parents met in the 1950s. From an early age, my brothers and I understood the value of education, and that we would also attend college was never in doubt. Like United Methodism, Unitarian Universalism requires its clergy to have a formal theological education—which is often not the case in Pentecostalism. Unlike United Methodism or Pentecostalism, Unitarian Universalism offers the opportunity to be part of a religious movement unconstrained by false doctrines, including prohibitions against LGBTQ clergy, of which I would have been one.

I began to imagine being the leader of a different kind of congregation than the ones I'd seen—a thriving congregation that combined an exuberant worship style, which I had experienced and been deeply moved by within some African-American churches, and the freedom of individuals to define faith on their own terms, which I was beginning to appreciate within Unitarian Universalism. With that vision in mind, I cast my lot with Unitarian Universalism as the larger institutional framework from which such a congregation could be built. Twenty years later, I have served several remarkable congregations of different sizes, locations and means, but I have never been the leader of a congregation that closely matched what I had originally imagined.

In more recent years, I have become a member of the Unitarian Universalist Association Congregational Life staff, helping local congregations, their ministers, and their lay leaders work toward *interconnection, innovation,* and *impact.* Our intention is that these ideas become guiding principles in this work, such that the growth of our relationships deepens our sense of interconnection; the new relationships and situations in which we find ourselves call us to innovate; and, through strong bonds with one another and the courage to try new things, we will have an impact—that is, we will make a difference in the lives of others. If I have a hope for our liberal religious tradition early in the twenty-first century, it can be summed up in these three concepts.

Interconnection

The signs of hope I see in Unitarian Universalism have to do with our ability to authentically connect with people who for whatever reason may never join our congregations. Two examples of this come from my three years as a minister at the Unitarian Universalist Church of Arlington, Virginia. I began working at the congregation in 2010, the summer that our General Assembly voted to go forward with meeting in Phoenix in 2012, even though Arizona governor Jan Brewer had just signed SB 1070 into law. At the time these were the most stringent measures to discourage undocumented immigration into the United States. Some of our Arizona congregations had allied themselves with immigrant advocacy groups who in turn invited the Unitarian Universalist Association en masse to stand for justice with them in 2012. This led to the first ever "Justice GA," where we focused more on our support for Arizona's undocumented residents than on the inner workings of our association. I took to heart Moderator Gini Courter's call to engage deeply with immigration as a moral issue and went to Northern Virginia committed to make a difference.

As the minister with primary responsibility for guiding the congregation's justice work, I collaborated with a team of dedicated lay leaders and activists to organize community events and town-hall meetings on immigration. We had a book discussion group. I led a worship service for Martin Luther King Jr. Sunday called "Dreamers and the Dream," which made the connection between King's famous speech and the dreams of the "Dreamers"—youth and young adults who came to the United States undocumented or who overstayed their visas. Many of these young people have excelled academically, but are denied access to in-state tuition to further their education because of their immigration status. Over the course of my tenure, the Arlington church developed a relationship with the Dream Project of Virginia and its Dream Scholars. Members of the congregation now serve on the Dream Project board and help raise funds for scholarships. The church is the site of many trainings and support gatherings for the Dreamers as they learn to advocate for themselves.

At the farewell dinner the church hosted for me at the end of my time there, one Dreamer mentioned in her remarks that when one of her friends asked her where she was going that evening, she replied, "I'm going to my church." She acknowledged that while she was not a member of the congregation in any formal way, the Unitarian Universalist congregation was, in fact, where she was most known, where she attended events, where she returned again and again. If there was a church where she belonged, the Unitarian Universalist church was it.

The second experience has to do with a connection made during our focus on immigration as a moral issue. A leader of an immigration advocacy organization was looking for a place to hold an immigration summit. He approached my colleague Linda Olson Peebles and me, and we agreed that the Arlington church would host it at minimal charge. That relationship continued to grow over the years, and when that leader and his wife had their first child, they chose to have her dedicated in the Unitarian Universalist church, where she could grow up loved for who she is, free from the gender-based limitations of the tradition in which her father had been raised.

These two stories point in the direction I hope our denomination will go. In them I see relationships formed over time in the context of meaningful, collaborative work for justice. I see a Unitarian Universalist congregation opening itself to be of service and finding common cause with people beyond its membership. In doing so, it has engendered connections and relevance that might not have otherwise existed.

In my current work as a member of the field staff, I often have the privilege to stand for justice and compassion with small-town Unitarian Universalists, including those who advocated for marriage equality before it became the law of the land. One early connection I made was with the Campaign for Southern Equality, an organization promoting full recognition of same-sex marriages in

Southern states. Its leaders helped same-sex couples and their allies organize, particularly through their "We Do" campaign, in which those couples, surrounded by a crowd of loving witnesses, went to apply for marriage licenses or to have their marriage licenses from other states and countries filed by their local county clerks. Among those working for marriage equality in the South, Unitarian Universalists consistently showed up as partners in the struggle. Our connection with people and groups outside our congregations help people find us as we join hands to work toward justice for all. I feel hopeful when we partner with other organizations who share our convictions and commitments.

Innovation

The new and renewed ways of approaching our worship services is another sign of hope. I am particularly encouraged by the work happening in groups such as Sanctuary Boston and the Sanctuaries of Washington, DC, where young adults are leading themselves and others in centering, reflecting, singing, praying, and sending forth. I had the chance to provide some assistance with such a service during the 2014 General Assembly in Providence. Thousands of Unitarian Universalists joined in that heartfelt, energetic worship experience that reflected our celebration of life as we prepared to join Rhode Islanders in the streets of the city for WaterFire, its recurring street festival. I suspect that the reasons that worship service seemed to resonate for so many had to do with the strength of the worship leaders and their coordination, the smooth transitions from one portion of the service to the other, the vulnerability of the speakers who shared reflections, and the encouragement of congregational participation. I personally felt so enriched at the end of that service that I began imagining some Unitarian Universalists attending such a large-scale service once a month rather than a less energetic Sunday service week after week.

I am continually inspired by the examples we have of multisite ministries—those in which congregations share resources, staff, and services. Among the most inspiring to me is the history of All Souls Church in Washington, DC, and the congregations around the city that were started at the end of World War II. Rev. A. Powell Davies and his leaders had a vision of a Unitarian church on each of the major roadways leading into the city. At a time of gasoline rationing, it became impractical for members of All Souls who lived in Northern Virginia to trek into the heart of DC for worship. So they used the modern technology of their day—land lines and intercoms—to transmit Davies's sermons out to the suburbs in real time. Arlington was the first of five congregations to get started that way, and from those five emerged three *more* congregations.

Today we have congregations that are carrying forward the legacy of innovation demonstrated by those Unitarians and Unitarian Universalists in metropolitan DC. First Unitarian Universalist Church of Houston and the First Unitarian Church of Albuquerque now have satellites of their main campuses. The Church of the Larger Fellowship has shifted from primarily a "sermons-by-mail" service in years past to a vibrant collection of communities that brings people together remotely, including through weekly video programs and a prison ministry. As I write, groups of Unitarian Universalists are gathering virtually to explore the possibility of ministries without walls, reaching people far beyond congregations' physical buildings.

As our modes of communication continue to evolve, so will our ways of being in religious community. Each new platform brings with it opportunities and challenges. Social networks allow us to communicate instantly with many people, but there are those who choose not to be online on any of those platforms. A notice in the printed newsletter was sufficient to get the word out about a congregational event decades ago, but how do we reach as many people as possible in the many ways they receive messages? Innovation can also imply the renewing of our minds such that we commit to ongoing engagement with our ever-changing electronic media landscape.

In more recent months, as Unitarian Universalist congregations have become more engaged with the Black Lives Matter movement, we have seen the power of electronic media to connect communities as well as facilitate their creation. Unitarian Universalists on Facebook and Twitter use those platforms to organize and promote actions in solidarity with black people. Online talk shows like *The VUU*, produced by the Church of the Larger Fellowship, create virtual venues that bring us together for important conversations about racism, resistance, and resilience. New Facebook groups like "Black Lives of UU" and the "Congregation for Black Lives"—both operating outside the official purview of our UUA—create spaces for healing, learning, and inspiration. These new ways of being a congregation were inconceivable for most of us twenty years ago. Now, the Internet makes it possible for black Unitarian Universalists with Internet access to gather among themselves and with allies across time zones and the limitations of their local congregations.

Another place I find hope is in long-standing organizations that have reimagined themselves. When I was in divinity school, I participated in a program of the National Conference of Christians and Jews (NCCJ) called Seminarians Interacting. It provided a valuable context for theological students from liberal, moderate, and conservative Jewish and Christian seminaries to experience each other's worship and learn from each other's traditions. As far back as the early 1990s, NCCJ was considering the new name it eventually adopted: the National Conference for Community and Justice. Seeing how the world had changed since its founding in the battle against anti-Semitism in 1927, and how its own mission and vision had evolved in light of that, NCCJ took on a new identity while carrying forward its commitment to kinship and fairness among all people, regardless of ethnicity or religious affiliation.

Like NCCJ, the Unitarian Universalist Association is far removed from the origins of its name. That distance has implications for our relevance in the public sphere. How might we honor the legacy we have received as religious liberals while boldly reinventing our tradition in this modern era? What sacrifices are we willing to make regarding our institutional identity so that others can more easily discover the richness of our communities? Where are the bridges between how we have known ourselves and how we may yet be? Those sacrifices to come and those bridges to be built are all part of our commitment to innovation.

Impact

I am filled with admiration and respect for communities in the South that have maintained a Unitarian Universalist presence in an environment often hostile to religious traditions perceived as foreign. Many of these congregations have paid a price for having been so far ahead of their time. During the civil rights era, some received multiple bomb threats as they stood for integration of public spaces and voting rights for African Americans.[1] In the twenty-first century, we have already seen congregations in the South targeted for violence and disruption on Sunday mornings because of our affirmation of a woman's right to choose when she will have a baby and our commitment to equality for gay, lesbian, bisexual, and transgender people. While such attacks are rare, the reach of fundamentalist Christianity throughout the South does make Unitarian Universalists there stand out in significant ways. Some congregations play down the radically inclusive nature of our tradition in order to fit in with their neighboring congregations. Some are content to be sanctuaries and gathering places for liberal-minded people—often from other parts of the country—who have learned that church affiliation is a social requirement in the South.

In spite of these challenges, we continue to bear witness and tell new stories about our faith. We know that people are hungry for our message of inclusion, freedom, and love. Those of us who come from other traditions imagine what our lives might have

---

1   Gordon Gibson, *Southern Witness: Unitarians and Universalists in the Civil Rights Era* (Boston: Skinner House Books, 2015).

been like had we known of Unitarian Universalism earlier. Some of us go as far as to say that Unitarian Universalism saved our lives. It is humbling to work for an organization where people say that with deep conviction.

In some ways, Unitarian Universalism has been wildly successful, if we consider how the values affirmed by Unitarian Universalists have found their way to the heart of life in the United States. Our seven Principles seem to become more relevant over the generations, with the advancement of civil rights for African Americans, the women's movement, the green movement, marriage equality, LGBTQ rights, immigration reform, and Black Lives Matter. While victories in the struggle for justice are never final, we can nonetheless be grateful for the distance we've traveled over the past fifty years.

As long as there is religious bigotry, zealots who will take the lives of others in the name of God, and youth cast aside by their families because they choose to have sex with a person of their same gender identity, there will be the need for liberal religious institutions. As long as there are believers who want to require prayer in public spheres and deny women the right to choose to have children or not based on theological mandates, there will be need for liberal religious institutions. Unitarian Universalism is probably as valid an institution as any for promotion of liberal religious values, even with its too-long name, complex organizational structure, and heavy reliance on white, middle-class Eurocentric norms for much of its identity.

Recent findings from the task force to reimagine the Episcopal Church are relevant to other denominations, including the Unitarian Universalist Association. They state national denominational structures can do little to reverse the trend of dwindling Sunday attendance and congregational membership. The power to reverse course lies in the congregations themselves, which must adapt and transform within their particularized contexts. While UUA staff can assist and advise in the process, UUA congregations—traditional and otherwise—will be leading the way.

The two strands of our faith emerged from movements that ran counter to the orthodoxy of their time and geographical context. Where people were being told that God would send them to hell for not confessing Jesus as Lord and Savior, Universalism emerged with a message of the love of God that extends beyond the limitations of Christianity to every human being, such that no one who accepted its truth had to fear damnation again. Where people were being compelled to believe that God could be known only in three manifestations—Father, Son and Holy Spirit—Unitarianism emerged to underscore and affirm reason and the indivisible nature of divinity. Over time, those two movements continued to evolve and change, still keeping their inclusive, noncreedal foundations, which allowed non-theists to join their numbers.

Now, two hundred years after those movements took root in North America, we are far removed from their original contexts and *raisons d'être*. Through scientific inquiry, we comprehend much more about our bodies and the rest of the universe. We can tell new stories about how diseases are transmitted, rather than interpreting them as curses. Through global genetic mapping, we can trace the migration of human beings out of East Africa to the farthest reaches of globe. We have ventured to the moon and used technology to get up close and personal with other planets and galaxies. While many continue to believe in a god that stands outside creation and controls human activity based on prayers and praise, others have come to embrace a different view, one in which if there is a capital-G God, then that God is indeed inseparable from that which God has created. Still others have no use for God in any form. When Unitarian Universalists practice our deepest values, there is room for all these people under the big tent of Unitarian Universalism.

That being said, we live in a world where the lines of distinction among denominations are disappearing and attendance at congregations is decreasing in general. Over the last decade, we've watched the "rise of the nones"—the growing number of adults who eschew affiliation with any religious organization. Giving to congregations is down, and many who claim to be "spiritual but not religious" are taking their spiritual pursuits to private retreat centers, self-actualizing weekends, and hiking trails. People attend congregations less and less based on their traditional ties to the doctrines of specific denominations and more on their affinity for the congregation's minister, the services it offers (for example, a strong religious education program for children and youth or social outreach), or the style of worship. Many questions arise with this information.

A parallel story regarding historically black colleges and universities also raises relevant questions. I am a grateful and proud graduate of Howard University, so much so that I have not one but two degrees (Bachelor of Business Administration and Master of Divinity) from the "Mecca of Black Education." Colleges and universities like my alma mater emerged as a response to the systemic racism that shut African Americans out of public schools like the University of Mississippi. Both my brothers are UM graduates now. Barriers that our parents faced in the 1950s did not exist for us in the 1970s and 80s. Our hometown, which had not one but two historically black colleges for most of the twentieth century, was down to one black college by the turn of the millennium. Now that the legal blockades to education for African Americans are gone, do we still need historically black colleges and universities (HBCUs)?

No and yes. As long as racism dictates that mostly white police from outside African-American communities can descend upon darker-skinned people in those communities and treat otherwise peaceful people as hostile combatants, we will need the counter-vailing presence of HBCUs. As long as African-American people are presumed guilty of whatever crime they probably didn't commit, we will need institutions where African Americans can be educated. As long as black women scholars are "presumed incompetent," to borrow from the title of a recent book on racism and sexism in academia, we will need institutions where young black women can learn, where their intelligence is not deemed intrinsically inferior to that of their white male counterparts.

On the other hand, many African-American students have taken on the challenge of getting an education at predominately white colleges and universities. While there will always be a need for schools that maintain their strong identification as African American, statistics indicate a need for fewer of them simply because African-American students have more options than before. So what might become of those HBCUs that have closed or are on the verge of closing? In my fantasy, at least some of them could become private institutions dedicated to the new population of disenfranchised students—the Dreamers I mentioned earlier. More than a few excel academically in their public high schools and want to be productive citizens in the only homeland they have known. However, they have been shut out of college in their home states because they can't pay exorbitant out-of-state tuition. What if just a fraction of the struggling HBCUs turned their attention toward *those* disenfranchised students? What might the impact be on the Dreamers, on the communities where those schools are located, on relationships between those schools and the families of those students?

Similarly, if Unitarian Universalists are to have an impact in the twenty-first century, we will need to invest in new relationships and dare to experiment. We can take a cue from our predecessors who distinguished themselves from what they had been taught and charted a new course. If we take to heart the idea that revelation is not sealed, to paraphrase Unitarian Universalist theologian James Luther Adams, we will live our lives as testimonies to our faith, like so many who have gone before us. What could have more impact than that?

During a three-year break from ministry work around the turn of the millennium, I got my real estate license in Massachusetts. I didn't make a lot of money, though I did learn a term or two that served me well once I came back into the parish. One of those terms was *adaptive reuse*—taking an existing structure built for one purpose and updating it to be used for another. The factory building at 24 Farnsworth Street in Boston that the Unitarian Universalist Association now has as its office spaces is a perfect example.

We can see how adaptive reuse applies to our Unitarian Universalist identity. It's been a long time since *Unitarian* in our movement was used to distinguish those who did not believe in Trinitarian doctrine from those who did. It's been a good many decades since *Universalist* in our tradition was used to distinguish those who believed in salvation for all people from those who did not. Yet we've retained these terms and even conjoined them, as we seek to imbue them with new meaning and relevance.

Some of our congregations and the buildings that house them predate the founding of our country, yet we now have a generation of young adults that prefers access over ownership—that is, many would rather borrow or rent a car on the rare occasions they need one rather than to own one. Similarly with congregations: The sense of ownership that membership implies doesn't resonate in the same way today as it did for young adults of generations past.

I find hope in the young adults who are stepping forward and bringing new energy to Unitarian Universalist congregations while discerning for themselves how much they are willing to invest in them. Like Unitarian Universalists before them, they want to make a difference in the world, to be inspired, and to contribute. Unlike those who have gone before, they don't have as much patience with systems and bureaucracies that move slowly and thereby support the status quo.

My hope for the reimagining of Unitarian Universalism is deeply rooted in trust—trust among congregations, trust between congregations and the larger Unitarian Universalist Association, trust between longtime Unitarian Universalists and newcomers to the faith. Trust can be earned over time, and sometimes trust is granted before it is earned. That kind of trust ties back to faith. As we are reminded in the Christian scriptures, "Faith is the substance of things hoped for, the evidence of things not seen" (Hebrews 11:1). In the bold new world of the twenty-first century, when advances in technology are reshaping our lives and our livelihoods at an ever-increasing pace, we will need to have faith in each other, sometimes based on our belief in each other's inherent worth and dignity. We will also need to have faith in the Source that holds us all and in the story that wants to be told through our efforts. Congregations will come and go, as will ministers, organizations, technologies, and songs. The manifestations of our long history might be as unrecognizable to us at the end of the twenty-first century as we ourselves would be to those at the end of the nineteenth. Through it all, we can find hope in the constant threads of interconnected relationships, the courage to try new things, and our commitment to making a difference.

Unitarian Universalist Military Chaplaincy and the Promise of Pluralism

REBEKAH A. MONTGOMERY

"Ma'am, I want to use the military chapel for a Wiccan ceremony," a service member with a defiant look in his eye declared to me one day. "Okay, great," I responded. "Let's talk about what you need. My assistant here will help us with the logistics." I offered a warm smile and gestured for him to sit down. He had a puzzled look on his face but sat down. "Ma'am, I said Wiccan—like Pagan. That's okay?" I had anticipated this request after reviewing the general faith trends of the unit and hearing from other service members of the various worship circles in our ranks. "Sergeant, not only is it okay, it is my responsibility to ensure, as much as possible, that you have the time and space you need to celebrate your faith." And thus began our conversation as to how to make that happen.

As a military chaplain, I encounter service members from every corner of this country and from around the world. The military is inherently pluralistic and multicultural. Every religious and spiritual path fills our formations, as do agnostics, atheists, and those of unaffiliated spiritualities. All are welcome to seek out chaplains for counseling, whatever the issue may be. Military chapels are also nondenominational and not affiliated with any specific religious tradition. The chapel opens its doors to provide a worship space for any group that requests, and so standing religious symbols or sacred items are not displayed permanently in any military chapel.

The worship space is to remain neutral and flexible, therefore making it a dynamic space for service members to use to deepen their connection with their faith. Many use the chapels for reflection and meditation, as a place of quiet and solitude. One of my sacred roles is to ensure the religious freedom of our service members and to encourage them in their spiritual traditions, as the mission permits. Of course, that caveat is unique. For example, a Jewish service member may not be able to keep the Sabbath if we are in the field or there is an emergency. We strive to balance the missions with making available opportunities for religious observances, which sustain the inner resources of each person.

My service as a military chaplain informs and supports my faith as a Unitarian Universalist. I also see that the military embodies much of our shared reality of coexisting in a pluralistic and multicultural society, where getting to know my troops and their families means also inviting dialogue about their religious and spiritual traditions, how they understand the sacred in this world. This interdependent web of all existence is not only a reality in UU congregations but among our troops as well. As we strive for diversity and wholeness, our faith tradition reflects our potential to realize the diversity of the vast spectrum of humanity and to live out the promises of Beloved Community. For me, serving in the military in such a diverse and pluralistic environment means facing daily the traditions and heart yearnings of a vast spectrum of beliefs. I support and serve Jewish, Pagan, Christian, Humanist, Buddhist, Voodoo, Hindu, Native, Sikh, atheist, and agnostic service members equally, as each asks to be supported. Service members seek out chaplains to wrestle with faith and life questions, and while we may not share their faith, we take the time to understand and sympathize with their struggles and problems. We provide them with resources to sustain their spiritual lives and engage in thoughtful reflection. We represent an immense diversity of thought and identities. And yet, we serve together, we worship together, and we build communities. Nowhere else but the US military do people of such diverse backgrounds work and live in such close proximity for such extended periods, and chaplains are on the frontlines of serving these communities with humility and great heart and love. And so we share with our colleagues and UU congregations our valuable lessons in serving in a pluralistic environment as a way of guiding us toward our shared vision for our faith tradition.

When that young service member came to me seeking support for the Wiccan group, at the root of his request was a challenge: Will you accept me? In affirming support for his professed faith, military chaplains communicate to him and those of each faith tradition that, yes, we accept you and respect you, and you are welcome in our midst. The military has a long way to go to accept and celebrate all service members. For me, however, the seeds of pluralism as a reality and a source for creative interchange and building the Beloved Community are here. Just as in Unitarian Universalist congregations, chaplains here communicate to those who seek our communities, "No matter who you are, you are welcome." Our words of welcome in worship often encompass the totality of human existence: hearts, souls, minds, bodies, pains, joys, sufferings, hopes, and dreams.

Affirming Our Shared Principles

So how do we celebrate pluralism and the diversity of beliefs in UU congregations? First, we affirm the common language of our hearts, as expressed in our seven Principles and the Sources of our living tradition. In our shared professed Principles, which foster in our communities those ideals we strive to embody, we hold sacred "the inherent worth and dignity of every person" who calls our congregation home. And as a military chaplain, I particularly carry with me our Fourth Principle describing the "free and responsible search for truth and meaning" to my service. All who enlist or commission into the armed forces have their own search for truth and meaning as they navigate what it means to serve as well as exist in our society as a spouse, family member, friend, and human being.

All service members must wrestle with what they experience at home and abroad, confronting at times what can be considered the worst of human nature: senseless violence, destruction, failures of diplomacy that lead to international military conflicts, terrorism, genocide, and so much more. My chaplain colleagues are by and large much more socially and theologically conservative and traditional than I. Yet we come together to serve and sustain our flocks with a common passion and dedication that goes beyond denominational affiliation. Just as in our congregations, each person we worship with brings their entire lived experience into our communities, seeking wholeness, healing, and fellowship. Living our shared Principles with intention begins by bringing into our precious keeping all those who call our congregations home.

Getting Comfortable with Being Uncomfortable

A second way to celebrate pluralism and the diversity of beliefs in our congregations is by becoming comfortable with being uncomfortable. In our congregations and worship services, we may hear sermons, prayers, and discussions that touch tender places in our spirits because of our own experiences. A congregant at a large Unitarian Universalist congregation once came to me after worship to tell me she was upset because I chose to use too much "God language" in my sermon. Another congregant once told me that I used too many illustrations that focused on women. Another congregant told me I used too few about women. After years of ordained ministry and worship with dozens of UU congregations, I can affirm that we are truly a diverse association of congregations. Sitting with this idea of pluralism as a reality and a promise means for me examining and reflecting upon where discomfort comes from. For some Unitarian Universalists, there are pains and hurts from the faith tradition of their childhood; for others, it is the systematic injustices perpetuated in the name of religion and the traditional patriarchal and hegemonic reinforcement of oppressive gender roles and dictates around sexual orientation. For others, it is the complexity of a multicultural and ethnic society and the generations of prejudice and violence associated with oppression. As we affirm our shared Principles, we are also charged with the responsibility to respect each other's beliefs and experiences. By reflecting on our individual paths on this earth thus far, we parse out those complex areas of where others' freedom of spiritual expression and our discomfort meet.

My service as a military chaplain is incredibly challenging for some of my Unitarian Universalist brothers and sisters. In meeting this discomfort, it is the prayer of my heart that others experience the ways my military chaplain colleagues and I bring the hope, love, and healing of each of our faith traditions to the wider world. As a part of the Principle of working toward global peace, liberty, and justice for all existence, there are Unitarian Universalists who feel called to assist members of the military with religious, spiritual, and emotional support. While every UU military chaplain brings her or his own sense of calling to the ministry, I look to the past, present, and our future to affirm mine. As a part of our shared history, the founder and forefather of Universalism, John Murray, was a military chaplain. Two Unitarian Universalists have served as the secretary of defense of the United States. Our Principle of the inherent worth and dignity of every person fostered the creation of the Geneva Conventions, which assert that human life is precious even in war and armed conflicts. As a human species we have not evolved past the need for a standing army to protect and defend nations and peoples around the world. While I pray for peace daily and for wisdom and discernment for our world leaders, I know that there must be those who are willing to serve and perhaps die to defend and avert catastrophic loss. People from every walk of life feel called to such service, and thus it is my honor to walk alongside them, sustain their spirits, and heal their wounds, regardless of their faith tradition, regardless of who or what they are. The sacred motto of the chaplain corps also names our three core competencies: to nurture the living, comfort the dying, and honor the fallen. Similarly, Unitarian Universalist congregations nurture and care for the living regardless of what lies in the deep caves of their hearts, regardless of their spiritual path, regardless of their ethnicity, race, sexual orientation, income, age, or ability. The promise of living and loving one another in this rich, diverse context carries on in our present circumstances and as we plant the seeds of a more peaceful world of tomorrow.

Suspending Judgment

In order to truly celebrate pluralism as that which binds us in love to one another, we need to suspend judgment. Christian pastor Joel Osteen states, "Your job is not to judge. Your job is not to figure out if someone deserves something. Your job is to lift the fallen, to restore the broken, and to heal the hurting." As a military chaplain, I do not use judgment as a tool for my ministry. Each person approaches me with her or his own identity, and it is my responsibility to adjust and adapt to build the bonds that extend a warm welcome. I have a dear friend who was raised in a strongly humanist Unitarian Universalist congregation. He confided in me that as a young person singing in his high school and college choir, he couldn't bring himself to even sing the word *God* or *Jesus*, and he struggled with the reality that UU theists and Christians are part of our living tradition. As such, he found it challenging to make friends who followed a spiritual path different from his and would confront UU theists as being irrational and simpleminded. He confessed to me one day that he was unkind and even cruel. At times, over coffee after Sunday services, he would dismiss and insult others. With tears streaming down his face, he came to realize that he was no different from those who hold racist, sexist, xenophobic, and homophobic beliefs. My dear friend, with this painful insight ripping at his heart, faced that his inability to hold in his precious keeping the inherent worth and dignity of all people was ultimately destroying his spiritual identity as a Unitarian Universalist. He concluded that he was no different from a parent who rejects a child for being LGBTQ; no different from someone who ends a friendship with a person in an interracial relationship. Thus he sowed the seeds of his recovery and continued his growth as an integrated person of faith. Suspending judgment in our faith tradition means affirming the importance of radical love and acceptance as the ultimate expression of how to live together in community.

The drum beat of my heart relays the perpetual message to others that you are precious, as you are created and called to be in this world. As a faith tradition looking to our vision of tomorrow, we can be buoyed by the reality that the beautiful gift of pluralism is alive and thriving in our congregations and we indeed have the skills to recognize and celebrate it. In affirming our Principles, getting comfortable with being uncomfortable, and suspending judgment, we ignite the hope that diverse worship communities will shine the light of Unitarian Universalism into a bruised and hurting world. If you feel welcome in this community, how do you welcome others into our precious keeping? The philosopher Lao Tsu reminds us that peace in the world begins with peace in the nations. Peace in the nations begins with peace in our communities. Peace in our communities begins with peace with in our homes. Peace in our homes begins with peace in our hearts. As we find and lift up that peace, may we each be charged with extending that peace to all those we call kin and celebrating the promise of pluralism and diversity in our midst.

A Story of Imagination

MARK STRINGER

The call came from the UUA offices in Boston in the spring of 2001. In a few days I would be spending a week with First Unitarian Church of Des Moines to discern with the congregation whether I would be their next settled minister. The caller didn't want to discourage me, but he thought I needed to know the truth. "Some people are unhappy with the search committee," he said. "They are saying the church needs a minister with experience." He didn't know how many people comprised the "some," but he did know that tension was growing and that I should arrive prepared for it.

I was not surprised to receive this call. I knew the congregation had been sharing ideas with the interim minister that had sparked their imagination—ideas of who they could be in the world. I knew the core leadership didn't seek to merely break through a thirty-year membership plateau of 250 members; they wanted to rocket past it, doubling the number of members within a few years' time. And I knew the story of how their lay leaders paraded through the sanctuary during a service the previous year chanting, "Five hundred five in '05!" Growing Unitarian Universalism had become their mission and rallying cry. They deserved to have a minister with experience. However, experience in ministry was not something I would be bringing to Des Moines. I was a seminary student still a month away from graduating. I hadn't even been a Unitarian Universalist for five years yet. Perhaps my exuberance for the congregation's growth goals was distracting me from my deficiencies. What did I really know about growing a church?

I phoned the chair of the search committee. He expressed the committee's confidence in its selection of me. He said they had been telling those who were unhappy to withhold judgment, saying, "Wait until you meet him." I was grateful for their support. I, too, believed I was the right minister for them. I reminded myself that the future success of the congregation depended less on what I would bring and more on what we could bring out in each other. The experience we would most need for our ministry was not the experience I lacked but the experience we would gain together.

Sure enough, we shared a foundational experience for our future just a few days later.

One of the first members who visited with me during the drop-in hours of my candidating week told me that he was "mad as hell" at the search committee for choosing a minister without experience and that he wasn't supporting my candidacy. I didn't seek to change his mind or to prove my worth. I listened and told him I understood. Later that week, gathering with leaders, I heard their concerns about the grumbling of this fellow and others like him. "Should we ask them to stop it?" someone wondered. We decided a better approach would be to assure those who were unhappy that they would have a chance to voice their concerns in the congregational meeting before the vote. When the member who had visited with me earlier that week received his assurance call, he said, "I've changed my mind. I'm going to vote yes." When asked why, he responded, "Because I met him."

What a relief it was for the core leadership and for me when the congregation called me in a nearly unanimous vote! Together we risked imagining a future that was different from what we initially expected. And then we chose to move toward that future, even amid uncertainty. The search committee needed imagination to risk going against the congregation's explicit instructions to call a minister with experience. I needed imagination to withstand the discomfort I felt as I learned that some were disappointed with the committee's choice. And, most of all, the members needed imagination to accept that the best match might not be what they had initially convinced themselves they wanted.

The triumph of the imagination we all showed in these pivotal early days would take a few years to be fully realized. Nevertheless, I believe that beginning our relationship with this kind of risk taking did lay the groundwork for our future success. We learned that we didn't need to fear dissent. We could leave space for it, seeking to preserve relationships even when we knew we might not agree. We could choose to hear disgruntled voices with compassion and understanding, carefully considering their perspectives. And then we could make the best, most future-focused decisions we could imagine.

Upon my arrival as the settled minister that fall, we immediately made another of these decisions, changing the early service time to coincide with the much-revered Sunday forum. Again, some people were unhappy, believing that the forum should stand alone. But with the congregation's clarity on growing the church, we had to imagine that things could happen simultaneously, that everyone would not be able to attend everything, and that would have to be okay.

Next, inspired by the understanding that churches would grow larger only if they offer opportunities for small church experiences, we sought to create a small group ministry program. I didn't know how to do this and neither did they. So we learned together. I recruited a team of twelve people, including longtime members and brand new folks. We considered together the published descriptions of different approaches, grateful for the work of Glenn Turner, Bob Hill, Calvin Dame, and others. And then, every two weeks for six months, we shared a small group experience that modeled what we had come to agree we wanted—to nurture meaningful connections by creating space to share from our lives and reflect together on questions at the heart of what it means to be human.

In the spring of that first year we rolled out the program to the congregation with the motto "Meaningful connections—ten people at a time." More than a third of the church participated, drawn to the enthusiasm we shared from our own experiences of the approach. Unlike some of the other small group models we had studied, our program expected groups to end every six months, with another enrollment period and six-month session to follow. Limited commitments helped with facilitator recruitment and enabled participants to alter meeting times to accommodate their ever-changing schedules. And, we found, the more we switched things up, the more meaningful connections could be made. We also learned that involving newcomers in decision making and leadership has significant benefits. After all, who better to help discern new directions to follow than those who are the least attached to the old ways?

By the end of my second year in Des Moines, we decided to choose another new direction by joining AMOS, our local congregation-based community organizing effort. Just a few years earlier, devoting 1 percent of the congregation's operating budget to organizational dues that funded interfaith justice work would have been controversial, if not impossible. But now we were embracing the promise of pluralism. We were focusing more on the gifts of new relationships than the challenges. We were trusting that we could learn from and create positive change with people of other faiths, even when the rituals and language of those faiths made some of us uncomfortable. And we were operating more in accordance with the promise of generosity—not only in our financial commitment to this work, but in our confidence that we could navigate any challenges that might arise if AMOS took sides on issues which the congregation did not fully support. Our decision to join AMOS further showed that the congregation no longer expected to unanimously agree in order to act.

With several of our core leaders participating in AMOS trainings and actions, the disciplines of organizing became woven into the fabric of our congregational life—the value of nurturing relationships, the necessity of hearing and learning from marginalized voices, the emphasis on identifying and encouraging future lead-ers. Together we experienced how effective organizing involves trial and error, persistent action and evaluation, and focusing on the world as it should be rather than being resigned to the world as it is. Participating with AMOS not only provided the opportunity to live our values more broadly in the world. It also taught us how to be a more effective church.

Another expression of the promise of generosity emerged in our early years of ministry together: expanding our welcome to those who visited our church. As a relative newcomer to Unitarian Universalism myself, I had been dismayed by the lack of atten-tion paid to guests in our congregations. A young adult who had served as board president my first year agreed. She volunteered to become a visitor coordinator, serving in that role for more than a year without pay, modeling for the congregation the impact that could be experienced when we treated our guests as though we really wanted them there. By 2004, we transitioned this role to a staff position, a new member coordinator who would direct the systems by which we traveled with newcomers from their first visit through their first six months of membership. This ten-hour-a-week position was more than worth the investment. We went from just a few new members a year to 5 to 10 percent annual member-ship growth, a rate that continues today.

With the church now growing as we had hoped, and plans afoot for the first capital campaign in fifty years, I found myself getting anxious. Now I was the one worried about my lack of expe-rience. I knew there were many things we could be doing better. Certainly I could gain some knowledge that would enable me to help the church navigate the growing pains we were experienc-ing. I traveled to an Alban Institute workshop called "Maximizing Potential in the Medium-Sized Church" with a long list of how-to questions and a yearning that I would return with answers.

I didn't get the answers there I thought I wanted, but I did get the answer I most needed: Focusing too much on *how* to do things can inhibit the imagination that is invited when we ask questions rooted in *why* we should do things. I learned that, as organizational consultant Peter Block has written, "the answer to how is yes."

Around the same time, I consulted with a wise colleague in town, a minister with more than thirty years of experience. After acknowledging that in my work as a minister I felt unsure of myself much of the time, I asked him when I would know that I know what I am doing. He said, "It's an interesting question, but I think it is not one I would ask. Ministry," he explained, "is intentionally going to the places where you can't possibly know what you are doing."

I decided to embrace my not knowing as a strategy and encouraged the congregation to do the same. I began holding "church chats" every few weeks on Saturday mornings or week-nights. Everyone was welcome to attend, but I extended personal invitations to a mix of established and emerging leaders. I would stand at the front of the room with a flip chart, and I would ask the two dozen or so attendees to share the tensions they felt in their experience of our church, the things that they didn't understand or yearned to see improved. Many of the concerns raised had grown from our willingness to let things fall apart. Even as membership in the church was growing, attendance at Sunday services was increasing, and we had raised $1.3 million to update and expand our church facility, committees were having trouble recruiting members and mostly stopped meeting. Meanwhile, the children's religious education program was foundering, buckling under the weight of our own success, and the forum no longer existed, driven to extinction by a lack of leadership and attendance.

As folks shared their complaints, confusions, and disappoint-ments, I wrote down responses, asked follow-up questions, and did my best to be a nonanxious presence. Difficult though it was, I resisted the impulse to defend, justify, or explain so that I could leave space for the leaders to hear each other and to offer their perspectives to the mix. We all had to employ a spirit of gener-osity to tell each other the truth about the life of our church and to hear that truth without moving to blame or attempting to problem-solve too quickly.

At one church chat, a member decried the lack of what she referred to as "tall trees"—established church members upon which emerging leaders could lean when faced with questions or challenging situations. As I looked around the room, I saw many people who already were these tall trees, but who didn't know it yet because we hadn't created the structure that would enable them to serve and be seen in that way. It was a nut that would take a few more years to crack.

These church chats were not just sessions for complaining. They opened up important why questions that led us to consider new angles on the challenges we faced. Acknowledging that no one knew for sure what would work and that everything we tried would be an experiment, we generated lots of new ideas for ways we could be better together, ideas that emerged from members hearing each other's concerns and passions and choosing to work together to attempt solutions. Not all the ideas would be successful; this we knew. But we believed that being imaginative in our approach would teach us things we otherwise would not know. Through these meetings we changed service times, reorganized our religious education programs, shifted congregational priorities, and discerned together the need for clearer lines of authority and responsibility. We were learning and growing together by embracing the unknown with generosity and imagination. Still, even bigger changes were to come.

As a project of my sabbatical in 2008, I visited larger Unitarian Universalist congregations, seeking to observe the challenges and successes they experienced as they had navigated growth. While I found no one-approach-fits-all answers to common problems, I did draw some conclusions about church governance and staffing that would inform the next steps we would take upon my return to Des Moines.

Throughout the first eight years of my ministry, I had been perplexed by the role of the board. Beyond financial oversight and a best-guess approach to budgeting, the board seemed to have little impact on the life of the church. Many were the years when the board would hold a retreat, write down on newsprint their hopes and dreams for the congregation, and then affix colored stickers next to the ideas to which they were most drawn. And then, for the most part, nothing directly related to this prioritization would happen. Even as board members were liaisons to the committees, they held no authority over what these committees did. Some years the perspectives of the chair or its most anxious members dominated the meetings of the board. Other years the board was preoccupied with emotional process in the church, not knowing what else to do. Despite the good intentions of everyone involved, board service appeared to be an inefficient and ineffective use of some of the most talented and devoted members of the church. Coordination of church programming toward commonly agreed upon goals was virtually impossible.

The larger congregations I visited on my sabbatical all employed a policy governance approach. In these congregations the board was expected to create policy, define expectations, and monitor results, including holding the executive-level staff accountable for the overall performance of the church. This approach aimed to free the board to do the energizing work of articulating the vision and to free the minister, staff, and lay leaders to pursue that vision. Policy governance promised a means to get us to a new place: setting a vision and programming toward that vision.

I also discerned through my visits that rather than pursue the addition of a second minister, an expensive decision that would require clarity about delineation of roles and lines of authority that I didn't think our current form of governance would allow, we could make a wiser investment by adding to our administrative and program support staff. This would position us to more effectively meet the needs of our growing congregation and avoid a common pitfall I had observed in policy governance—minister burnout. I learned that once a congregation shifts to policy governance and the minister is held accountable to outcomes rather than to just preaching interesting sermons or being a nice person, the expectations and burden of responsibility can be significant.

Adequate staffing and systems through which this burden can be shared become essential.

Upon my return from sabbatical, I encouraged the board to consider with me the potential of policy governance. We did our homework and agreed it was the way to go, employing the services of consultants to help us with the transition.

At the same time, I gathered a team of church leaders to rethink our staffing, inviting them to imagine all the tasks that would be best handled by professional staff so that volunteers could be freed up to pursue fulfilling ministries rather than mundane duties. As a result of these conversations, we decided to further professionalize the roles and functions of our administrative staff, add a communications coordinator and assistants to our program staff positions, and plan for part-time youth and pastoral care coordinator positions. Looking at the costs of these changes, I could see we would need to raise our pledge income by at least 20 percent in the first year alone. I got cold feet. I told the team I didn't think we could do it. One of them said, "Mark, tell us what we need. We'll find the money." As other team members nodded in agreement, I remembered another important lesson that a colleague had once shared with me. He said, "The minister's job is to ask the question. The congregation's job is to answer."

So, I kept my cold feet to myself. I celebrated with the congregation when we did raise the money, and I delighted as we hired the additional staff I knew we would require as a growing congregation employing a policy governance approach.

Seeking to lighten the burden on me that I expected from a new governance approach, I started talking to church leaders to gauge interest in a new group that would serve as lay staff to oversee vital areas of church life—the "tall trees" members had told me we needed. I was particularly interested in having past board members serve, those folks who had been in the upper levels of leadership of the church and who I knew had wisdom to share, but who sometimes struggled to find their place in leadership once their board service had concluded. Within a few months, I had commitments from seven church members who met with me to discuss the goals of this group, the various positions we would need, and the covenant we would share. Thus, the Council for Congregational Ministries was formed, with councilors overseeing ministries of congregational life, stewardship, building and grounds, religious growth and learning, worship and arts, social justice, and communication. The covenant we crafted explains the purpose of the group well:

> We seek to nurture and promote the health and vitality of our church. Therefore, we covenant to thoughtfully engage with the church staff and the volunteers in our assigned ministries in pursuit of the ends articulated by the Board of Trustees.

We will:

- work together as a council to support excellent communication, activity coordination, and committee task alignment across all the elements of congregational life.

- nurture leadership within our areas of ministry and within the council itself.

- challenge our assumptions and presumptions of how things are or need to be and reach for creative ideas and solutions.

- seek to empower volunteers whenever possible according to the Iron Rule: "Never do for others what they can do for themselves."

- attend our scheduled meetings, prepared to share the joys and concerns of our ministries.

- recruit a replacement should we decide to retire from the council.

- hold each other accountable toward the goals of this covenant.

The councilors serve by the invitation of the minister only as long as they are energized by the role and the relationship is working. I craft the agenda for the monthly meetings, which are run as small group ministry sessions with generous time for thoughtful reflection. We talk each other through congregational challenges, celebrate successes, and grow our relationships to one another in the process. Our church has been well served by the work of the council and I can't imagine attempting policy governance without them.

Five years in, our new approach to governance now affects decision making in every area of church life, including in 2014 the hiring of Rev. Erin Gingrich as our first associate minister of social justice. A recent all-church survey revealed that 83 percent of our congregation agrees that our "mission and vision drive church decisions," an astounding result given that just a few years earlier few people in our church even knew we had a mission and vision!

Our congregation's story of urgency contains plentiful evidence of the trinity of promises celebrated in this book. We would not have been able to grow the church were it not for the imagination shown by a core group of leaders and their inexperienced minister who saw the potential of Unitarian Universalism in Des Moines and who dedicated themselves to bringing that potential to life. We would not have welcomed hundreds of new Unitarian Universalists into our congregation during this time were it not for the willingness of our membership to open itself to the pluralism of new people and new perspectives, even as we maintained respectful connections with our past. And we would not have had the leadership resources or the staff team necessary to help us pursue our ambitions were it not for the generosity of our membership, who continue to share their time, talent, and treasure from a place of abundance rather than scarcity.

Our story may strike you as an outlier. As you reflect on the history and current circumstances of your congregation, you may assume that the changes we have experienced in Des Moines would not be possible in your setting. And you may be right. However, if members of our congregation had been polled during the thirty-year membership plateau that preceded the ministry we have shared, I'm guessing many of them may have dismissed this story too, resigned to the low expectations that contributed to the congregation's limitations. Only when a core group of members decided to step forward and lead with confidence could things change. Only when they took the chance to embrace a vision of future vibrancy could that vision be realized. Only when these dedicated women and men chose to live the promises of our faith could they grow the church and grow themselves in the process. Might there be a core group of leaders in your congregation willing to take similar risks? Might you be one of those leaders?

We have had our challenges along the way, just as any congregation will. Not all the approaches we have tried have gone well. Many times we have had to return to the lesson we learned at the beginning of my ministry—the need to provide space for disgruntled members to be heard, to carefully consider their questions and critiques, and then to move forward the best we can, with imagination and integrity. We've had to cultivate flexibility in our expectations, learning through trial and error that growing a congregation requires not only imagination of what could be but also generosity of spirit when we fall short. And we have learned over and over that the experience we most need comes not from knowing exactly how to do things but in the imagination we employ in asking why it matters that we try, in the pluralism we invite as we welcome as many voices as possible to participate, and in the generosity of spirit we invoke as we remind ourselves that what makes our work together ministry is our willingness to intentionally go to the places where we can't possibly know what to do.

With the structures and staffing now in place, we are well positioned to be the vibrant Unitarian Universalist congregation we have always dreamed of being and the vital liberal religious community Des Moines deserves. When a congregation embodies the promises of imagination, pluralism, and generosity, anything is possible.

LIVING THE PROMISES

The essays in this book call for a renewed and renewing story about how we and others know Unitarian Universalism. The Beloved Community that Unitarian Universalism aspires to be holds "the promise to one another [of] our mutual trust and support," as stated in our Principles document. The Beloved Community is the doctrine of church that every Unitarian Universalist congregation and program can and must live into.

I am not suggesting that we abandon our historic commitment to justice making in the world. But isn't it hypocritical and incongruent for us to shape the world with our vision of the Beloved Community, yet be unable or unwilling to do the same when it comes to the congregations and programs we serve? As Beloved Communities, we can model our vision for the larger world, including the future generations of Unitarian Universalists. "Why," asked theologian Howard Thurman, "has the church been such a tragic witness to its own Gospel?"[1] What must we do to become the Beloved Community? What must happen to shape this ecclesiology? How will we embrace and leverage a covenant of trust and support to break through an ossified and shrinking iChurch? The essays in this section are a glimpse of what could be.

---

1 Howard Thurman, *A Strange Freedom: The Best of Howard Thurman on Religious Experience and Public Life*, ed. Walter Earl Fluker and Catherine Tumber (Boston: Beacon Press, 1998), 254.

The authors describe shared ministries and congregations that fill the gap by restorying our faith and moving Unitarian Universalists farther from iChurch and closer to Beloved Community. In short, these shared ministries are restorying and birthing the future of our faith.

The section begins with Ian Maher's provocative and challenging essay about the congregation he helped establish and formerly served, Original Blessing in Brooklyn, New York. This congregation came together around the interdependent messages of Universalism, God's love for all people and the Seventh Principle of Unitarian Universalism, proclaiming "the interdependent web of all existence." These are at the core of Original Blessing—they comprise the original blessings of life, shaped by a holy, grace-filled generosity that is now threatened by global climate change—and have led to their reimagining of Unitarian Universalism. This essay describes the congregation's and Ian's ministries and their mission to be in right relationship with the creative force of life (God)" and with the communities they serve. Erik Martinez Resly also writes of the "congregation" he serves, yet, other than sharing an urban setting and being Unitarian Universalist in origin, the Sanctuaries (Washington, DC) is very different from Original Blessing. Resly's essay describes the arts ministry shared by the participants he serves, a "congregation" that passionately believes, lives, and performs their theology as a spirituality of the arts, often on the streets of Washington, DC. Like Original Blessing and the Sanctuaries, the Lucy Stone Cooperative is also unlike most conventional Unitarian Universalist ministries; but it too is built on and living the promises of Beloved Community. Heather Concannon and Rowan Van Ness walk us through the development of this imaginative and diverse shared ministry that led to a dynamic cooperative housing model that for many is the kind of community they seek, one that makes sense in the twenty-first century.

The Sanctuary Boston—like the others in this section—developed as a promise. David Ruffin describes how generosity, pluralism, and imagination gave direction to a deeper and sustaining hope: the need for a Unitarian Universalist faith community that some—primarily young adults—couldn't find at more traditional worship services. This essay takes us from the inception of the congregation through its change in leadership, a critical transition in the life of new groups.

Like the Sanctuaries, AWAKE Ministries in Annapolis, Maryland, also started as a promise deeply shaped by generosity, pluralism, and imagination. As described by Fredric Muir, John T. Crestwell Jr., and Christina Leone Tracy, it too has a dynamic, once-a-week worship service, but unlike the other shared ministries in this section, its target audience is intentionally multicultural and multigenerational. This ministry grew out of one congregation's commitment to the UUA's Journey Toward Wholeness and is supported by that spirit and the congregation's resources. AWAKE includes several ministries rooted in emotional literacy.

Kaaren Anderson, the senior minister at the First Unitarian Church in Rochester, New York, writes about her congregation's small group ministry program, which is enormous and touches nearly all of its members. Small group ministry and the connections it empowers are transforming, deepening, and growing lives; small group ministry has renewed and energized this congregation in meaningful and exciting ways. First Unitarian's story is a moving one and it's program can be adapted by any congregation. Nathan Alan Hollister has also built deep and sustainable Unitarian Universalist communities with small group ministry, but not in the context of a larger congregation. The final essay in this section describes the spread of "Sacred Fire" using models of praxis and justice-making that sustain each group's spirituality and pledging. It too is a remarkable and inspiring story.

Each of these ministries is unique by context and leadership. They are examples of where generous, pluralist, and imaginative thinking and leadership can lead. And versions of them—in particular or in general—are ministries that most congregations could live into. Each one began as an idea, a desire for something fuller and deeper in a Unitarian Universalist setting. Each has struggled to sustain itself. We might expect such struggle—giving birth to new life from the old is usually accompanied by disruption and discomfort. And they have persisted, thank goodness, for they are beacons of hope. Take to heart religious scholar Diana Butler Bass's words: "[This] is about the gap between a new spirit and institutions that have lost their way. Only leaders who can bridge this gap and transform their institutions will succeed in this emerging cultural economy."[2] The essays in this section bridge that gap. Let us all be so generous in our thinking and doing.

---

2 Diana Butler-Bass, "When Spirituality and Religion Collide," *USA Today*, April 15, 2012, 9A.

A Transformative Spiritual Relationship with the Divine

IAN WHITE MAHER

In the gray days of February 2012, seven people gathered in my living room for food, prayer, and conversation. Desire had brought us together—a desire for a spiritual community that could both challenge and support us as we listened to the call from the Divine asking us to transform our world. Over the course of that spring and summer, those seven people grew into what would become Original Blessing, the congregation I served as minister for three years. It is a congregation that has grown out of a great love for the history and legacy of Unitarian Universalism as a spiritual movement as well as a deep concern that what it currently offers, both theologically and culturally, is not enough to meet the challenges our world is facing.

We believe that the future of Unitarian Universalism depends upon becoming a transformative spiritual force committed to leading people out from the wilderness of individual prosperity and into the joy of communal intimacy and solidarity.[1] This movement begins by reimagining our faith communities as sites

---

1 At the time of this writing, I have recently left Original Blessing to work on a book about God and devotion. But the congregation continues to meet regularly, carrying out its mission. Here I use "we" to describe the community, its reasons for forming, and the good folks who continue their commitment to our vision.

of spiritual transformation committed to healing the world rather than as sanctuaries tucked away from it. Only by committing ourselves to a process of deep spiritual conversion will we be capable of resolving the environmental and social collapses occurring all around us. Our insistence on a commitment to disciplined spiritual transformation may upset some Unitarian Universalists, but ultimately, as a movement, we need to decide if we would rather directly participate in the work of salvation and love or resign ourselves to cosmetic changes that do not challenge who we are.

The Crisis

The world is facing an environmental collapse of such magnitude that many are now calling it the Sixth Extinction or the Holocene Extinction ("Holocene" refers to the present geological epoch), because its roots can be found in the rise of humanity. Unlike previous extinctions, the earth is now conscious of the massive climate change and species depletion. Humanity is the consciousness of the earth, and we are standing wide-eyed as we watch this extinction unfolding before us. Many blame the impending collapse on human *actions*, but this is only partially correct. The effects we are facing today (and tomorrow) are determined by our actions, but our actions are the products of the our decisions. The quality and condition of our decisions derive from our thinking. And our thinking is determined by our spiritual condition. To say the impending collapse is the consequence of our actions conveniently avoids our responsibility for our spiritual condition, which is the source of the cascade of all that follows.

This crisis is the ultimate consequence of the misaligned spiritual condition of human beings, which allows us to prioritize fulfilling short-term individual desires over short-term individual sacrifices that would provide long-term survival and prosperity for our species and other species. Scientific discoveries made over the past century have opened us to an exciting new awareness about our origins as living creatures. Yet we have lagged behind in shaping these new discoveries into a theological framework that helps us resolve the anxiety and alienation we feel. This propels us toward fulfilling individual desires and has contributed to the climate crisis.

The first step toward a solution is to admit that we are beyond the point of avoiding calamitous climate change. We cannot begin our process of transformation into healing beings without admitting that our spiritual estrangement has created an environment that will soon be unlivable for many creatures and, potentially, humans. The second step is admitting that we need help. Specifically, Original Blessing believes humanity needs help from the divine and creative life force that is greater than the selfish interests of our individual egos. Anything shy of this confession will leave us with the illusion that we will somehow, through our own will power and ingenuity, solve this problem. But we cannot solve a spiritual problem with intellectual solutions.

The Role of God

I am neither an atheist nor a theist. I define God as the creative life force, which is a fairly broad definition. Almost anyone can enter into that definition. But my experience has been that many Unitarian Universalists resist entering conversations or commitments that use the word *God*. They say, "There is no God," or "I don't believe in God." But what does this really mean? I agree that symbol of an old bearded man is wrong. I agree that a tremendous amount of harm has been done in the name of that bearded man. And yet, so many Unitarian Universalists cling to this old man in order to beat him up. We have become bullies of this feeble God and are missing the opportunity to stretch ourselves and encounter Creation. Our egos love this feeble, old God because we are able to enjoy the sense of personal power that comes from being self-righteous and clever. In our process of beating up this weak God, we have lost sight of the fact that we are not getting any closer to the authentic spiritual life that is needed to restore our mutilated planet. So we must ask ourselves, "Do we want to be right or do we want to survive?"

The resistance of Unitarian Universalists (and many others who are unaffiliated with organized religion) to encounter or even discuss God is understandable. We live in a culture defined by fear, scarcity, and isolation. Often what is offered as a spiritual resource in this culture is shame-based religion that idolizes a demanding but fickle God who regulates his people through punishment and force. As an alternative, we UUs sometimes adopt one of the various prosperity gospels that champion and elevate the individual experience both spiritually and socially, which can result in an odd, narcissistic, spiritual isolation.

When the word *God* is used, it is often called offensive to the ideals of Unitarian Universalism. But it is really only offensive to the ideals of a particular Unitarian Universalism that has become primary over the past several decades, the one in which the individual dominates. This is unfortunate. This is the individual run rampant. This is the individual as tyrant.

If we are willing to release the feeble God from our clutches and lift our heads up to look around, we might find that believing in God is not difficult at all. If we are willing to allow ourselves to be opened by an encounter with Creation through a practice of surrender, rather than relying on a spiritual life guided by self-determined will, we will be amazed by the mystery that opens to us.

At Original Blessing we feel called to help people experience God—the creative life force—and to restore a sacred relationship with our planet. We are saying, "Wake up, wake up! Put down your ego. Submit to transformation." We believe that our survival as a species, and the survival of so many other species, relies on more religion, not less. And it is contingent upon a religion that asks us to practice, praise, and worship not for our own benefit but for the benefit of others. It is a style of worship that asks us to surrender our drive to fulfill our own spiritual needs and, instead, to seek out worship that aims to fulfill the spiritual needs of others.

Reimagining Our Story as a Spiritual Transformation

In Unitarian Universalism, there is an unexamined culture (as opposed to a faith position) that is best defined as being the religion where "you can think whatever you want." When this cultural value gets challenged, people become upset. Many people attend Unitarian Universalist congregations because they have found communities of people like them. This is the reification of the individual, a spiritual home that tells you that you are okay just as you are. The only real problem is we are not okay. We are really not okay. The world is falling apart. Those people out there are not the problem. We are the problem. Or part of it, anyway.

It is not that Unitarian Universalists can't do things to help ameliorate our climate and social problems. We can. But Unitarian Universalism is not up to the task of resolving the cause of our climate and social problems, which is the misalignment of our spiritual condition. In this sense, this essay is not about the climate but about transforming the misaligned spirit through spiritual discipline. My experience is that, as a faith movement, we ask little from members regarding developing a spiritual devotion capable of transforming one's character. The idea that we need to radically change what, why, and how we express spirituality in worship will disrupt many Unitarian Universalist congregations who may insist that there must be another way to address the impending calamity. But without a deep spiritual surrender that releases us from what we pretend to already know, we will not have the capacity to change our thinking and our perspective for understanding the world around us.

Unitarian Universalists are very attached to our current form of worship, but it is not preparing us for the future. The challenge for us is not the particular actions we take but the spiritual condition from which all the actions derive. Because the impetus for the environmental collapse is spiritual and not intellectual, it is impossible for it to be diverted by smart people who come up with the right scientific solution. Original Blessing believes that the impending collapse will be resolved by people who are willing to actively seek an experience of transcendent interdependence with the planet and who ask to be transformed by the creative force called God. And for Unitarian Universalists, this cannot happen until we reconcile ourselves with what God is and transform our misaligned spirits through spiritual discipline.

The spiritual life of many Unitarian Universalist congregations can be characterized by statements like "I finally found people who think like me," or "When I found this congregation I felt like I had come home." Of course, finding a spiritual home where we are comfortable and nurtured is important, but what is troubling and implied by this statement is that the end of the spiritual path has already been achieved. But if we are going to contribute, then we need to be more than sanctuaries away from the world where people can feel comfortable. We must change ourselves. We must change ourselves or we will die. As upsetting as it may sound, many Unitarian Universalist congregations are presently not up to the task of being houses of spiritual transformation, because we have not decided that we want to be houses of transformation. We want to be houses of comfort and nurture.

In positioning ourselves as the alternative to the shame-based religions and myths, we Unitarian Universalists have cultivated a spiritual environment that approximates the prosperity gospel churches, with their heavy reliance on individual salvation. Our conversion to and worship of individualism is so complete and compelling that it is often invisible to the dominant culture within Unitarian Universalism. We speak of interdependence, but in practice our worship and our spiritual expectations, for the most part, actually reinforce an isolated spiritual experience. We say things like "We walk together on our separate paths," but when pressed, we find it hard to articulate where exactly the promised land we are walking to lies. Much of our practiced spirituality suggests that our relationship to the sacred is intensely personal and not in any way dependent upon the spiritual development of others. That is, a person's ability to experience transformation depends upon their willingness and dedication alone. In this situation, my spiritual life is not affected by another person's spiritual exile. But this is just not true.

Praise Is Our Path

Original Blessing believes that we are all connected in God and that the intimacy of our spiritual condition depends upon the spiritual health of all the people around us. We cannot as isolated beings experience the spiritual awakening that waits for us. To the extent that we understand ourselves as separate entities, we demonstrate that we do not understand the actual nature of who we really are.

The Original Blessing community is driven by a desire to praise the beautiful world we grew out of, just as the grass grew out of it. We are a mystic congregation, meaning we believe that the desire we feel for a deeper spiritual connection is God's desire for us. We are desired by Creation. The loneliness we feel is God's loneliness for us. We are wanted by Creation. The joy that we feel is God's joy for us. We are celebrated by Creation. We are not isolated beings whose experience is bound by the limits of our epidermis. We are part of a great cosmic experience, and our spiritual calling is to seek transformation in order to come back into alignment with God, the greater life force.

We are looking for a positive spiritual direction that is not defined by the traditional religious narratives, but we are also uninterested in communities that seem to exist only to talk about why these myths are false. We want spiritual development. We want a path that helps us become healers of the planet.

The spiritual experience of being evangelicals in the world, offering a path into a new spiritual condition and helping us face the future as humanity approaches possible extinction, is calling us. We cannot afford to sit in our sanctuaries, distanced from the world, and talk about slavery, prisons, wars, dying oceans, and melting glaciers. We can no longer afford to stand by as our kin live without experiencing the transcendent love that undergirds all life.

Thousands of religious liberals will gather for protests, yet it is difficult to gather two people to go into the street to talk about the sacredness of our lives and the call to a sacred purpose. Yet the experience of love and joy that can hold both our happiness and their sorrow, of blessing in this world despite our imperfections, brokenness, flaws, anger, and fear, is a powerful message of ultimate importance. By reclaiming the experience of joy, we come into spiritual solidarity with all life. Spiritual intimacy and solidarity with all life is found in the transcendent experience of this saving message.

Original Blessing's mission statement reads, "We are a spiritually ambitious movement seeking a relationship with God in order to transform our world through creative worship, social justice, and compassionate community." What do we mean by "spiritually ambitious"? In so many religious communities a high value is placed on humility, which seems to run counter to the idea of ambition. Ambition is often defined as being willing to do unscrupulous things to get ahead, taking more than one's share, and being driven by a desire for fame or power. Original Blessing, doesn't understand ambition in this way. Our emphasis on spiritual ambition recognizes a communal need and inclination in which we experience a greater sense of connection and faith as a body rather than as individuals. Our spiritual practice is done not for our own benefit but for the benefit of the people around us. We must work on our spiritual lives if we want other people and future generations to live better lives. Given what we know about the coming environmental crisis caused by climate change, we feel a mounting urgency to get serious about our spiritual condition. We are ambitious in the sense of understanding where we want to go and in working together to arrive there as a community.

We are not engaged in this spiritual ambition so we can share in a personal sense of serenity or cultivate a unique and privileged relationship with God. We believe God does not work that way. A return to God is a return to the base of all being. That return is the process of both losing the limitations we have placed on our understanding of ourselves and encountering that which defies name and number and boundary. When we understand ourselves as the earth, not intellectually as many Unitarian Universalists already do, but spiritually, we will cease to litter the earth with our waste and exploit it for our short-term comfort. We hunger not for personal enlightenment but for the enlightenment of humanity, and praise of Creation is the path we choose. Original Blessing places our communal relationship with God first. We pray together. We dance together as a form of praise. We believe that learning songs by heart is essential to a robust spiritual life, so we don't use hymnals or projected hymns. We teach every song by shouting out the lyrics and then repeating the same song four weeks in a row. And then we come back to the same music six months later. Every service has five to six hymns. As a result, we have a loud, singing congregation of people who use this music in their everyday lives. We train our members to testify about their faith experiences from the pulpit. We regularly hold events in public spaces where we can introduce ourselves to our neighbors and they can learn about what our congregation offers. Our purpose as a community is not to be an inwardly focused sanctuary but an externally focused evangelical community that offers a spiritual message about communal identity and desire for God.

We Need Courage

It is unclear to me whether Unitarian Universalist congregations can radically change our spiritual mission from one that reinforces individualism to one that promotes the healing of others over the healing of ourselves. It is a lot to ask. Change is difficult. And the environmental calamity still seems somewhat unreal to many of us, even those of us who believe that it is coming. So the urgency to find a solution is still held only by a relative few. And among those few, the idea that the solution will be intellectual or technical remains dominant. However, because we do have an institutional structure (one-thousand-plus congregations) that allows us to speak to large numbers of people who, at a minimum, have a regular practice of coming to worship once a week, we are in a privileged space to be leaders in this movement, should we make the commitment to do so and then follow through with a program of action.

Many Unitarian Universalists are watching the climate change and the world's species become extinct, and we are aghast. This is not the future we want, and we know that we are the problem. But we have been content with blaming this crisis on human actions and behaviors and slow at addressing the source of the problem, our spiritual condition. In developing a transformative spiritual relationship with the Divine, one based on asking for help and surrendering to whatever that answer might be, we will inevitably encounter hurdles. We need strong visionary leaders who can chart a path for us over these hurdles and who can help us prioritize the transformation of our spiritual condition.

Unitarian Universalists feel a certain devotion to the democratic process, much of which I agree with. But our movement also expresses an impulsive and aggressive reaction to authority, likely derivative of our experiences with shame-based religions. Yet our survival depends on the courage and willingness of our leadership (clergy and lay) to risk careers and relationships in order to guide us into this new future. We will face a backlash from congregants satisfied with observing the coming disasters like present-day Cassandras, people who under no circumstances want the responsibility of the spiritual condition of their neighbors. Some of this will be painful, emotionally and spiritually. However, a radical change in our faith movement is not going to occur without people who are willing to take a stand against the hagiography of the individual and are willing to stand for a transformative spiritual experience that helps us worship communal being. At Original Blessing, this stance begins and ends with praise. It feels awkward to tell people that we praise Creation, because we don't want to be confused with "those people" and, perhaps, we don't fully believe it yet ourselves. But we are committed to working through our awkwardness, because the long-term goal of a sustainable future is more compelling than the short-term embarrassment of what people might think of us when we tell them that we are in love with God. It has not been easy, but we believe the journey is a life worth living.

*Visit **www.originalblessing.org**
to find out more about this community*

Art and the Future of Ministry

ERIK MARTÍNEZ RESLY

It was a clear Wednesday evening, surprisingly quiet for a weeknight in the city. The soft orange glow of the streetlights cascaded through the tall windows of the parlor at the Universalist National Memorial Church of Washington, DC, where we were gathered for the first of our two monthly Huddles. While other clusters of returning artists were scattered throughout the building to solicit feedback on their personal learning goals, I sat in a circle of roughly eight people, all first-time visitors to our spiritually diverse arts community. We were sharing original paintings, songs, photographs, and other forms of creative expression, when our eyes shifted to Kevin, a younger black man who had remained quiet up until that point. Without uttering a word, he reached into his pocket and pulled out a crumpled piece of paper. He proceeded to unfold the note, revealing a maze of doodles and scribbles. "This is something I wrote," he muddled, shifting nervously in the chair, his glance cast downward toward the scrap of paper now resting in his lap. The group waited for Kevin to break the silence, but he held his tongue.

"Would you mind if I read it?" a female voice inquired from the other side of the circle. We turned to meet her eyes. It was an audacious proposition. "Sure," Kevin responded, "if you want to." The white woman extended her hand as Kevin scooped up the note from his lap and sent it leaping around the circle until it finally reached her outstretched fingers. She brought the paper close to her face, studied the ink marks for a moment, then began to recite these words:

> My talent yells at me! What are you waiting for? Why haven't you introduced me to your friends? Why don't you love me? I want to help the whole world, not just you. I need to interact and connect with other talents. I'm starving here! Dying of thirst! Feed me, put me where I can be exercised. Dress me up and present me to the world. I've been living in your shell for far too long. I love you. I need the same from you. I'm like the Doughboy in Ghost-Busters, I'm like Godzilla, I'm like King Kong, I'm a monster and I'm as big and dangerous as any city. I'm huge, I'm massive, I'm a part of you and since we share this life it's time we work together. Or we'll both die—inside. I'm not a demon but I'm no angel. I just am. I exist for you. I beg you—release me and watch life change.[1]

The circle erupted in applause as the last words leaped from her mouth. "That was good," Kevin said, smiling. "You read it good."

Something happened in that moment. Something changed. From that point on, I felt closer, more connected, more intertwined with the other bodies in that room. We were present to one another in a deeper way. You might say the group came alive together. Looking back, it is significant that this scene unfolded in and through a poem. I would go so far as to say that the shift I experienced would not have occurred without it. The creative arts became the vehicle of ministry.

Yet, the creative arts were not cast in their usual roles: no handmade quilt to dress up the sanctuary, no handpicked hymns to reinforce the sermon message, no theatrical props to dramatize the worship theme to children. From a production perspective,

---

1   Kev Harmon is a writer, who, in his own words, "goes back to the future or to the essence." Connect with him on Instagram @Harmonworld.

the aforementioned scene was amateur at best. We neither vetted our visitors to assess the appropriateness of their art nor consulted with a committee on how to arrange the lineup. We hadn't even rehearsed ahead of time. By all accounts, we fell desperately short of satisfying the criteria of professional excellence.

For many congregations, this standard of excellence has become normative and has amplified our attentiveness to the creative arts in ministry. We hire graphic designers to modernize our websites and recruit paid soloists to fill out our choirs. Some congregations show videos during worship or stream their worship as online video. While the turn toward excellence has helped prioritize the creative arts, it has simultaneously worked to pigeonhole them. Once valued as an end in themselves, the creative arts now largely operate as a form of ornamentation, embellishing the "real work" of ministry. We look to them to beautify spaces, illustrate sermons, and entertain children, but not to build community, fight for justice, or change lives. In short, the creative arts complement the more traditional arts of ministry, but they do not qualify as an art of ministry in their own right. What if they did?

Art in Ministry

One of the most daunting barriers to integrating the creative arts into ministry is the entrenched commitment to a narrowly defined vision of church. We have effectively allowed a single model of ministry to monopolize the term. In *Anti-Oedipus*, French philosopher Gilles Deleuze exposes the shortcomings of this logic by inviting us to imagine a "body without organs." The absurdity of the idea begs the question: What do we mean when we talk about a body? Typically we think of the body as an object, something unitary and stable. But it is equally if not more accurate to describe the body as a complex assemblage of organs that interact in specific ways to specific ends. According to this view, that which we refer to as a body is in fact the joining together of diverse elements into an apparent unity, which is then taken as its underlying identity. We assume that our organs exist to uphold our body, when in fact they are what produced it in the first place.

If this sounds rather abstract, let me offer a concrete example of this same logic at work in ministry. A Unitarian Universalist church in Texas had invited me to preach at their Sunday services, and in the sermon I referenced my colleague Ron Robinson's call to "broaden the bandwidth" on how we do ministry. After the service, an elderly white woman approached me and asked, "Are you saying that we should stop meeting on Sunday morning?" She was obviously quite unsettled by the prospect. "Not necessarily," I replied. "It depends on whom we're trying to serve. Sunday morning is convenient for some people and inconvenient for others." She listened carefully, respectfully, but couldn't hold back, eventually blurting out, "But if it's not on Sunday, it's not church!"

The image this woman had of church functioned in a similar way to our popular image of the body: something bound and fixed, a single object rather than a complex assemblage. To change the time of worship was to dispose of the order that gave it shape. By challenging her to rearrange the organs of the church, I threatened its very definition. It would have ceased to exist as such. "If you change the conditions that skin you," anthropologist Elizabeth Povinelli reminds us, "you will be un-skinned."[2]

These are the stakes when we imagine what new forms the creative arts might take in ministry. Decorating the body of our communities with rock bands and PowerPoint slides is simple enough. But what if we fundamentally rearrange its composition? Let me be clear: The image of a "body without organs" does not refer to a body that lacks organs so much as it depicts a body that lacks *definitive* organs. It is a body made up of organs that have not been organized once and for all. A "body without organs" invites us to imagine what other organisms might emerge were we to free our organs of the particular objects and aims to which societal rules have assigned them. For our purposes, let us loosely approximate

2   Elizabeth Povinelli, interview with Elizabeth Povinelli, www.elizabethpovinelli.com.

this idea using the concept of a church without ministries. This church might still retain the ministry of worship, but it would do so by liberating worship from its habitual chain of connection. For example, instead of fastening itself to the sermon, worship might plug into graffiti. Imagine the preacher spraying rather than saying her homily. Imagine the entire congregation tagging the sanctuary with words that arise for them in prayer. Many other trajectories could be followed, some closer to the popular image of church and others much farther away, yet each generating a different "body."

The Sanctuaries is the name our community has given to one such organism in flux. During the course of my studies at divinity school, I increasingly befriended individuals who felt disconnected from the more traditional forms of organized religion. Their reasons were eclectic, but their sense of frustration proved constant. When I moved to Washington, DC, after graduation, I set out to organize a spiritual community that would better serve their needs and fit their lifestyles. I felt a great deal of pressure at the beginning to define the final product. Donors required blueprints that would guarantee success. Local ministers sought clarity on the specifics of my model. In short, I found myself engulfed by requests for the answer at a time when I was still distilling the question.

I spent months meeting one on one with younger people across the city. We would gather in a local coffee shop or grab a drink after work at a bar. I was curious to hear when they felt most spiritually alive and how they might design a community with that purpose in mind. I had assumed going into these conversations that the challenge was primarily organizational. Would we hold worship in larger or smaller groups, on weekdays or weekends, with live or recorded music? But the more stories I heard, the more I came to realize that the very organs themselves were being shuffled. Some people spoke of mountain excursions and weeklong retreats, while others mentioned brunch outings and pickup basketball games. The most common and persistent theme, however, was the creative arts. Whether painting or singing, salsa dancing or pottery making, these younger people yearned to express themselves creatively.

Taking this realization to heart, I collaborated with a small team of volunteers to incorporate the arts into our first official gathering. We held the event on a Sunday evening in the loft of a dance studio. The liturgy bore striking resemblance to a more traditional worship service, opening with a spoken invocation, dancing from hymn to hymn, pausing for a brief reflection, and then closing with a communal blessing. Midway through, however, we incorporated a period of personal journaling, during which each participant responded to my sermon in poetic or visual form. Initially, the room sank into pregnant stillness, then erupted into "joyful noise" as participants exchanged stories and ideas with their neighbors. I sensed we had tapped something deep.

In the next incarnation of this new spiritual community, we experimented with a collection of smaller gatherings, each limited to eight people, which met at different times throughout the week in different neighborhoods across the city. These circles employed the arts as a form of spiritual practice. We composed prayers out of newspaper clippings, sang rounds written by members of the community, and created vision boards using magazine clippings. In addition, we began infusing creativity into larger justice-related events. We commemorated the legacy of Martin Luther King Jr. by inviting tourists to join us in composing poems on charcoal rubbings of his plaque on the steps of the Lincoln Memorial. In partnership with a local Methodist church, we cooked for our unhoused neighbors and designed table settings that extended blessings during the meal. It was clear that the creative arts had emerged as an important ministry in the body of our community.

Still, we struggled to organize ourselves. The transience of the population poached some of our most committed leaders. Money was tight, with many of our participants either unemployed or underemployed in a city infamous for inflated housing rates. Scheduling remained a constant challenge as public transportation delayed commutes and employers demanded unpredictable overtime hours. Our chaotic context required a creative response that only the arts could supply. We began to conceive of creative expression as the primary ministry feeding our community. Instead of devising clever ways to integrate the arts into the inherited organs of church, we asked, how might we nurture spiritually creative lives?

This question generated three distinct yet overlapping planes on which our community currently moves. On an individual level, our leaders equip the members of our community, or "artists," with the requisite materials and support so that they can work toward achieving their own spiritual and creative goals. On a communal level, we hold a variety of monthly gatherings that bring our artists together to build friendships across difference, to collaborate on artistic projects, and to reconnect with the sacred presence that sources and sustains their journeys. On a citywide level, we partner with small businesses and nonprofit organizations to create platforms for our artists to share their art in service of the city. These include, among others, performances at neighborhood festivals and justice rallies, open mic events that encourage first-time presenters to get up on stage, and pop-up gallery spaces that bring both beauty and patronage to local businesses. While this tripartite approach has allowed us to institutionalize our community to the point where leadership roles are clear and financial sustainability is possible, we have intentionally left room for the counterbalancing current of reorganization by empowering our artists to design and host their own ministries. Some lead workshops on prayer through photography, some teach classes on the spirituality of hip-hop, some stage house shows or perform on the street. In this way, we orient ourselves toward the "body without organs," an ever-shifting matrix of innovation, the very potency of possibility.

The more we experiment with new configurations, however, the less our church without ministries resembles the dominant model of church at all. I neither preach a sermon nor wear a stole nor reference a hymnal. We do not currently own a building and we have no intention of doing so in the near future. Our artists proudly identify with diverse religious traditions and some continue to attend their respective places of worship. Do we even count as a church? In collegial settings, I often find myself gently nudged into the cohort of "community ministers" faithfully serving in chaplaincy or nonprofit contexts. I gladly accept such designation. The lines of demarcation, we should remember, are hardly natural. Our definitions are derivatives, the products of an institutional lineage rather than their source. But to acknowledge the arbitrariness of the category "church" is not to dismiss the impact that it has on everyday life, its power as an illusion. The image of church carries real connotations that can animate or alienate. We have chosen not to conceptualize the Sanctuaries as a church, or for that matter as a synagogue or mosque or temple, but rather as an arts collaborative, thereby sacrificing symbolic, denominational, and financial resources in order to maintain our integrity as a community that falls outside the norm.

When we introduce the creative arts into ministry, we can never quite predict what will emerge. The body may reject its new organ, or the organ may fabricate a new body. Our community is but one particular expression of such surgical intervention. We have installed the creative arts as our central organ, not on account of their superiority to other organs but rather due to the unique work they perform. It is this distinct function to which we now turn.

Art as Ministry

Imagine a child who is afraid of the dark singing to calm himself down.

That image is an unexpected point of departure for an inquiry into the place and purpose of the creative arts. We tend to think of the arts in terms of radio singles and platinum albums, catchy refrains and production value, political commentaries or fashion statements. But the creative arts, Gilles Deleuze and his co-author, Felix Guattari, suggest, have little to do with what a verse means or what a painting depicts or what a sculpture represents. In the case of the frightened child, for example, we may never know the exact words he was humming, where the song came from, or whether he even got the lyrics right. Still, we can say with confidence that the song provided a "center in the heart of chaos."[3] Music soothed his nerves and stilled his soul. How is it that the creative arts command such force?

Conventional wisdom would have us focus on what a piece of art means. According to this line of thought, the power of art to transform the world arises from its power to convey a thought. Analogous to a foreign language, art is to be deciphered, then interpreted, so that its message can be understood. While I concede that the creative arts often communicate profound and provocative ideas, I am not convinced that they can or should be reduced to this role. We miss something essential about a dance sequence or spoken-word poem when we merely seek to explain them. Rather, they are to be experienced. Art arises out of and in response to chaos, the most bestial rather than the most abstract. The aforementioned child began singing because a shiver flashed down his spine and the hairs on the back of his neck suddenly stood on end. His agitation manifested itself on his flesh, in his flesh, at the level of matter. We can assume he confronted some intensity, a reaction in and on his body, which exceeded all intellectual control. It wasn't the idea of fear or horror so much as the scream he heard or the shadow he glimpsed that filled his body with a visceral sense of panic. The child sang because he sought an escape, he hoped the song might dry his tears and slow his pounding heart, not because he aspired to ruminate on the nature of darkness in lyrical form.

If we take this alternative approach to the creative arts seriously —that is, if we attend to how they awaken us to sensations and how they materialize in response to those sensations—then we can better appreciate their hold on humanity. They become as universal as the flesh itself, possibly even more, for the forces of sensation pulsate well beyond the human species into the farthest reaches of nonhuman life. In this way, the creative arts provide intimate and immediate access to those mysterious forces that animate ministry in the first place: the harrowing boom of a thunderstorm, the

---

3 Gilles Deleuze and Felix Guattari, *A Thousand Plateaus: Capitalism and Schizophrenia* (Minneapolis: University of Minnesota Press, 1980), 311.

piercing shriek of an infant, the towering grandeur of a mountain perched against the setting sun. They bespeak the Divine encountered, not merely interpreted or thought. The God of hair follicles on the human skin and gusting winds that echo through the city streets. The creative arts circumvent what everyday language loses in signification and translation. Instead of describing a phenomenon in abstract terms with ever-shifting meanings, they direct our attention toward it, that we might confront it ourselves in its raw intensity.

In the scene that inaugurates this essay, Kevin's poem was less an explanation of his internal struggle to claim his talent and more a direct immersion in it. I felt the tension in his muscles and the heaviness of his breath as I listened to the choppiness of his verse and the intonations that certain words demanded. His poem gave shape to what is otherwise incapable of being said, despite its striking ubiquity to the human condition. He had penetrated the chaotic undercurrents of our lives, a universality that does not transcend tradition and culture but rather flows at their root. The sensations Kevin's poem enacted and evoked can neither be contained within nor exhausted by a single identity, for they cut across identity itself. The creative arts, in this sense, are beholden to no one.

At the same time, this universality is always accessed in its particularity. Art does not exist in abstraction. It bespeaks a specific verse, a particular scribble, a singular pose. To make art is to conjoin, arrange, and contrast sensations using the materials at hand. It involves strokes of color and beats of sound, the interplay between textures and gestures, the eruption of new permutations. Here, individuality reigns. Each artist will conceive and construct a different frame, fusing personal technique with diverse influences and assorted bits of inspiration. Kevin's poem, for example, was uniquely his own, though it undoubtedly echoed stylistic patterns he had discovered elsewhere. The words he chose had been taught to him over the years. References to cult classics like *Ghostbusters* and Godzilla reflect the cultural era and milieu in which he came of age. His poem evidences traces of tradition and identity, which he inhabits in his own idiosyncratic way. This framing of chaos, this singularizing of multiplicity, is what allows the creative arts to hold diversity with such authenticity. It celebrates the individual and collective alike, the specific artist and her larger networks of identification, without erasing or fetishizing either one. I want to believe that this fragile balance, which is inherent in making art, helps to account for the wide range of racial and religious identities that comprise our community at the Sanctuaries.

Still, art does not stop at the frame. It is not meant to be static, something to hold or behold. The conventional impulse to interpret rests on the assumption that a piece of art contains a message like a bottle thrown out to sea. But the creative arts function more like the waves, pushing their listeners along, transporting their viewers to a shore yet unknown. In this way, we might say that art does not mean something so much as move someone. We are drawn into a theatrical scene, struck by a haunting photograph, moved by a heartfelt duet. The frightened child who burst out in song kept singing until he was carried by its tune into the arms of serenity. The creative arts activate us, reorient us, change us.

To engage the creative arts as ministry is to harness the power of transformation. Instead of debating which hymn supports the preacher's message, we must ask, Where will this song take us? Who will go with us? How else might we move in that direction together? The arts create a sacred space that renders the imperceptible perceptible. They become an access point to this world, our world, experienced anew.

If ministry is solely understood as a tool for making sense of our world, we would do better to consult historical studies, sociological surveys, and political analyses. But if we approach ministry as an invitation to explore new ways of navigating the world, new ways of living into the fullness of creation, then the creative arts open us up to becoming more. They remind us that we are always more than the closed image we have of ourselves. They compel us to sidestep our limited self-understanding and glimpse another side of who we could become. Kevin's poem illustrates this beautifully.

In the depths of his self-doubt, torn between the desire to express his talent and the dread of such exposure, art reached out through him. His poem called out for a reader, and the woman across the circle literally gave it voice. I like to think of that moment as one of mutual becoming, in which each person grew in and through the other without sacrificing selfhood. The Beloved Community, one might say, was in our midst.

Of course, one must be careful in such moments of mutuality not to collapse real structural differences between subjects. "Identities shape and ramify in worlds of social affiliation and care," Elizabeth Povinelli observes, "no matter the intentions of persons."[4] To simply wish a world of reciprocity is not enough. As a black man in urban America, Kevin faces different opportunities and obstacles than the white woman at the other end of the room, and vice versa. Our bodies remain socially coded in unjust systems of oppression. Our identities, while stripping some of power, can also secure some a heritage, a culture, a place otherwise denied. This paradox poses serious challenges to a model of ministry that uncritically promotes identity formation as its ultimate goal. Too often the heartfelt gesture to help someone grow in turn folds back into an imperialist attempt at growing them in our image. "Be more like us!" we shout, either unaware or unconcerned with the implications of such a demand.

The creative arts offer a way through this dilemma. Instead of pressuring individuals to exchange or adopt identities, they invite people to innovate within their own identities, testing their limits, exposing their excesses, uncovering their buried or latent possibilities. Which genres of music am I supposed to appreciate as a Chinese American? What responses do those photographs incite for me as a gay man? How many ways can I write a poem as a Muslim? These questions drive and derive from creative practices that, to quote Povinelli, "orient the subject to restless experimentation with the givenness of life, with how life might be

---

4   Elizabeth Povinelli, interview.

otherwise than it is."[5] To script a film is to imagine yourself into multiple perspectives on the same situation. To collaborate on a record is to adapt your playing to a different voice or a foreign rhythm. To be captivated by another person's painting is to feel the world through her frame on chaos, which then doubles back to disclose both the dimensions and the interstices of your own. The creative arts refocus ministry toward identity exploration rather than identity regulation. They work within and across identities, aimed not at hardening labels but bursting constraints that keep people small, self-satisfied, and self-contained. In theological terms, they challenge communities to avoid merely copying staid images of God. Instead, they make space for the invention of new pathways that reconnect us to the chaos, to that which is ultimate and primal, to the darkness that engenders a child's song and embraces his ensuing peace. The creative arts plunge us into the Deep, to borrow an image from constructive theologian Catherine Keller, where we come face to face with a God we may never fully grasp but somehow manage to touch in the moments we least expect.

Art of Ministry

On the first day of classes in divinity school, the dean of ministry studies addressed my incoming student cohort and clarified the goals of our three-year graduate education. We would certainly acquire knowledge, he explained, but of greater importance was the cultivation of "pastoral agility." To be effective religious leaders, we would have to learn how to navigate our way through situations beyond our control.

Ministry in this time calls for an unparalleled degree of agility. Religious leaders must think and act *with* the world, immersed as we are in its infinite unfolding. We may be tempted to try and slow the current, clawing for rocks underfoot and grasping for limbs overhead that will temporarily halt the flow. Perhaps this explains the

---

5 Elizabeth Povinelli, *The Empire of Love: Toward a Theory of Intimacy, Genealogy, and Carnality* (Durham, NC: Duke University Press 2006), 158.

typical approach to the creative arts to date. We have treated them as objects scattered along the path rather than the force that carries us forward. The creative arts possess the power, as I have suggested, to proliferate our practice of church and dilate our sense of self. They include not only the hymn sung in worship but the worship that bursts forth from the recording studio when four strangers share stories and join voices to create an anthem for justice in the city.

If we embrace the creative arts as a site of ministry rather than as a mere supplement to it, we will inevitably get swept up by the winds of inspiration. Spiritual community could take so many forms—if we let it. We must not confine these new directions in ministry, however, to the old dogmas we have imposed on ministry. It is a paradox that the greatest threat to ministerial experimentation is not that such efforts will be ignored by or excluded from the broader denominational gaze, but rather that they will be welcomed by and included in existing institutional structures exclusively on the latter's terms. As long as the traditional model of church remains the standard against which all other ministries are evaluated, I fear our well-intentioned efforts to promote and support entrepreneurship in ministry will likely fail.

Such failure would not only be bad for ministry, it would also be bad ministry. Let us not forget that the art of ministry is the pursuit of innovation itself, the extension of life to its limit, the opening of life into its fullness. The process is the point. And it is a process we must follow in faith, for we know not where it will take us, how it will change us, what transformation it will effect. The art of ministry begins with a single poem, scribbled on a piece of paper and stuffed into a pocket, that finds a reader on a Wednesday evening, builds a friendship against all odds, spawns a blog that inspires new writers, empowers a performance before a sprawling crowd, gives someone his voice.

Release me and watch life change.

Visit **www.thesanctuaries.org**
to find out more about this community

Better Together

ROWAN VAN NESS AND HEATHER CONCANNON

*May the door of this home be wide enough to receive all who hunger
for love, all who are lonely for fellowship. . . . May this house be, for
all who enter, the doorway to a richer and more meaningful life.*
—Adapted from *The New Mahzor*

Guests start trickling in shortly before seven, sometimes empty-handed and other times with food to share. A bell rings inviting everyone to gather in the kitchen, where we share names, preferred gender pronouns, a tour of the food on the table, and grace. We share a meal and conversation, before clearing dinner off the table and replacing it with desserts, candles, hymnals, and songbooks. Soon the house is alive with spirit and song.

Every Sunday night at the Lucy Stone Cooperative, we gather for dinner and singing in one of the shared spiritual practices of our community. Five years earlier, there was no Sunday night gathering but the seed of an idea that there might be a way to live together in community and incorporate our values more deeply into our daily lives. Today we live in an eleven-bedroom house, and share meals, chores, and decision-making, rooted in our Unitarian Universalist values and tradition.

The Lucy Stone Cooperative is in many ways a response to the social, ecological, and spiritual crises of our time. In a culture that feeds isolation, disconnection, and an unchecked consumption of resources, we believe that living in intentional community is a way to resist those forces—and that we can only resist them with the strength of our collective power and wisdom. We know that our faith calls us to a deep and inherent interdependence and we believe that we must create alternative structures and communities that make that interdependence visible. We are called to narrow the gap between the world as it is and the world as it might be, and this requires our boldness, imagination, cooperation, and spirit.

The Lucy Stone Cooperative is an intentional living community based on the values and tradition of Unitarian Universalism. In the summer of 2010, Unitarian Universalist Community Cooperatives (UUCC) incorporated as a nonprofit organization, and that winter purchased the three-story Victorian house known as the Lucy Stone Cooperative in the Roxbury neighborhood of Boston. The first housemates moved in after six weeks of renovations in February, 2011. Since then, the Lucy Stone Cooperative has been home to between eleven and fourteen housemates at a time, ranging in age from eleven to sixty-nine. Our community consists of people who identify as Unitarian Universalist and others who don't, but who are excited about living in a community with shared values and faith practices.

As an intentional living community, residents of the Lucy Stone Cooperative share meals, the cost of food and utilities, chore duties, and decision-making. Since moving in, we have completed a number of major renovations, built community within and beyond our walls, learned more about who we are as a community, spent time with our neighbors, had meetings and held parties, gardened, played games, laughed, celebrated, and mourned.

Alec Aman, a resident at the Lucy Stone Cooperative, says,

Cooperative living provides me with an accessible and recurrent opportunity to intentionally engage in a mutual exploration of the ecology of the human condition. It is the intimate and often mundane daily interactions with different and differentiated people and relationships that create fertile ground for better understanding the complexity of those around me, and through them, understanding more about myself.

UUCC and the Lucy Stone Cooperative share three core values: spiritual practice, sustainability, and social change. We try to live these out and are consistently interpreting and reinterpreting what they mean for us. For example, we benefit from the sustainability of economies of scale through buying bulk food and having one washer and dryer for twelve people. But how do we bring sustainability into our renovations when weighing it against other values, such as keeping the rent affordable? How do we bring social change and justice into our relationships with one another and the wider community we live in? How can we share spiritual practices in a way that builds community, without requiring everyone to participate? These are all questions we are living into and asking as a community as we seek to build intentional, faithful, and spirit-led communities.

Barbara Seidl, a former resident of the Lucy Stone Cooperative, says,

> Living in community was, for me, an exercise in which even the most abstract concepts came to life in the blood, flesh, and bones of my housemates. Cooperation, fear, commitment, frustration, and democracy were not concepts. They lived at the dinner table and in house meeting. They were there, present, in the room, to be addressed rather than theorized. Fear was what brought our ability to make decisions to a halt. Cooperation was what allowed us to serve thirty guests with two hours' notice. Frustration was the tears in my housemate's eyes as I unwittingly disappointed her, again. Commitment was what made us both stay at the table to talk it out, again.

We purchased the Lucy Stone Cooperative property using community-supported financing, through an arrangement known as the group equity model of cooperative home ownership. In this model, the equity stays with the nonprofit organization instead of accumulating for the housemates. Housemates pay rent to UUCC, and over time, the equity accrues for the purpose of maintenance and expanding the organization through the purchase of additional properties, allowing more people to live cooperatively. While many cooperatives work with banks, we were thrilled to purchase the property for $375,000 through a mortgage with the Cooperative Fund of New England, an organization that predominantly loans money to worker cooperatives. We borrowed $140,000 for our down payment and initial renovations from eleven individuals, one congregation, and the Unitarian Universalist Association (UUA). These smaller, community-financed loans, ranging from $5,000 to $25,000, were made at a lower interest rate, and for a shorter period of time, than our commercial mortgage, allowing more of the money raised from rent to go directly toward our mission rather than interest payments.

Each individual who lives in a property owned by UUCC is a voting member of the organization and purchases a member share of $500 to buy in to the cooperative. UUCC is governed by a board of directors, made up of UUCC members and community trustees, who are elected by the membership at an annual meeting each year. The board makes major fiduciary and governance decisions of UUCC and works on meeting organizational goals, whereas housemates at the Lucy Stone Cooperative make decisions about their shared space and community life.

UUCC's Beginnings

Intense, immersive experiences—such as retreats, summer camps, or intentional communities—are often transformative. Greg Buckland experienced the difference that cooperative life can make during his college years. Inspired by this, he and friend Matt

Meyer started dreaming about starting a housing cooperative. This dream began to take shape after they attended a workshop on how to start a new cooperative. The group equity financial model made starting the Lucy Stone Cooperative seem economically attainable for the first time.

At the time, the North American Students of Cooperation (NASCO), the national association of group equity cooperatives, had one member cooperative operating in eastern Massachusetts. The group equity model emerged as one way to keep housing affordable because of the low cost to join the cooperative and because the equity stays with the organization. According to the International Cooperative Alliance, a cooperative is "an autonomous association of persons united voluntarily to meet their common economic, social, and cultural needs and aspirations through a jointly-owned and democratically-controlled enterprise." The values of the cooperative movement align very closely with the seven Principles of Unitarian Universalism, and our justice work and UU faith have led us to believe that housing should primarily be a means for shelter rather than profit. In addition to member-owned cooperatives, Boston is also home to many rental cooperatives, as people are attracted to the economic, ecological, and social benefits of the cooperative movement. This, along with a concentration of Unitarian Universalist communities and networks, made Boston ripe for the creation of a new housing cooperative based on the values and tradition of Unitarian Universalism.

In May, 2009, a group of six came together at the Garden Street Cooperative in Lawrence, Massachusetts, for our first of many three-hour meetings. We were all in our twenties and thirties and were an intentionally racially and culturally diverse group, intending the leadership of the organization to reflect our hopes for the community we were creating. We ran our meetings democratically, sharing facilitation and using a modified consensus model of decision-making. Well before the first planning team meeting, Matt and Greg attended a cooperative training institute and began having a series of conversations with individuals to build networks and acquire any wisdom they could about cooperatives, fundraising, and creating successful communities. The planning team was well positioned to spend the first meeting getting to know one another, brainstorming a list of community values as well as needs, wants, and ideals for the property itself, deciding on a name for the cooperative, and coming up with a list of next steps.

After six months of organizing and planning, we held our kickoff fundraising party. With more than 180 people in attendance we were able to raise more than $14,000. The fundraiser was successful in large part due to the personal relationships we had built and the ways in which we continue to invite both Unitarian Universalists and the cooperative movement into a larger shared vision. The value of holding such an event went beyond the money we raised. The work of our one-on-one conversations had built energy and enthusiasm for our vision, and the great turnout renewed our sense of vision and purpose—we were truly addressing a need in our community.

Over the coming months, we continued to meet and began taking on the work of articulating our vision. We created a website, incorporated as a nonprofit, applied for a mortgage, wrote grant applications, and began sending out monthly newsletters. As a bold, new venture in intentional community, it was an important step for us to establish legitimacy for ourselves while simultaneously nurturing buy-in. It helped us develop our own sense of faith in what we were doing, especially as the stakes got higher and we felt accountable to the people who had given us money.

Rhythms developed in our meetings through check-ins and song. We lived into ways to hold one another accountable to the work we were committed to with grace and love. As we began to rely on each other more deeply, spiritual practices arose and became more evident. We actively reached out to one another to check in on our progress and to see whether people needed support in completing their tasks. We sang in moments of tension and uncertainty. We regularly and actively recommitted ourselves to our faith in each other and in this work.

Matt Meyer recalls the importance of shared spiritual practice in the process of purchasing a house,

> The process was an incredible adventure with success and challenges woven throughout. One of the most difficult times came right at the end of the process. We had found the perfect house. We made an offer, which was accepted, and we set a date to sign all the paperwork and close on the house. But the date was pushed back, and then pushed back again, and then again. We came together for a meeting to discuss our situation. It seemed that for reasons totally beyond our control, legal complexities on the seller's end, the whole thing might not work out. It looked like the two years of work might just slip through our fingers and there was nothing to be done except wait.
>
> We finished that meeting in a really hard place. There wasn't anything to do make our problems go away. There wasn't really anything to say. So someone suggested that we sing. We sang a song asking for guidance, "Guide my feet while I run this race, for I don't want to run this race in vain."
>
> When we finished singing, we took a deep breath together. We made eye contact with each person around the circle. Something had shifted. I recognized in that moment that the work of living our values in community and in relationship with each had already begun and would continue, whether we had a property or not.

After more than a year and a half of planning, organizing, meeting, worrying, wondering, and dreaming, we had incorporated UUCC, set a vision for this new community, gathered a community of support around us, raised over $150,000, made an offer, and, finally, closed on a property. We chose a group of twelve people who would become the founding housemates of the Lucy Stone Cooperative.

None of us has ever started a community like this before. We had never incorporated a nonprofit, purchased a house, or pulled together half a million dollars in financing. It was a leap of faith to do something this big. When we chose to put an offer on a house, not knowing whether people would actually apply to live there with us, we took a leap of faith. When we put our relationships on the line and asked people to donate money to our project, we took a leap of faith, as did the people who donated their money to us, trusting that we would use their money well, and that this dream would actually become a reality. And yet, without the trust, the risks, and the leaps of faith that were taken in hundreds of small and large ways, by our group and by our supporters, the Lucy Stone Cooperative never would have come into existence.

When new communities are dreamed into being, there is also an opportunity to create a new culture. Though we sometimes see ourselves slip into patterns of seeking security and certainty in uncertain times, we have tried to create a culture that supports generosity and abundance over greed and scarcity, spiritual groundedness over rushed decision-making, grace and compassion over anger and separation, and imagination and faithful risk-taking over restraint.

We had conversations, networks, and relationships before we had a website. We had shared values, culture, and spiritual practices before we ever wrote them down. We saw the ways in which our emerging vision spoke to people who came to our fundraisers, offered advice, and applied to live in the house. The community we have created is, in many ways, countercultural in an age that glorifies social media as the new and best way to build community, and yet we see the ways in which people are deeply hungry for real connections and spiritual community, for a faith that asks more of them, for communities that can see them through daily struggles, hold them accountable, and offer support in mundane and profound ways.

Organizational Growth and Development

After we purchased the Lucy Stone Cooperative and the house-mates had moved in, the planning team had an organizational question to consider. Now that the planning team had completed its mission of purchasing a property and selecting the first house-mates to move in, was there still a purpose for the planning team? The planning team gradually began functioning as the board of the nonprofit, and six months after we moved in, UUCC held the first annual meeting of its membership and formally elected a board of directors.

While the actual governance of the nonprofit was fairly straightforward, navigating the changing relationships, roles, and dreams that came with the birth of the Lucy Stone Cooperative proved difficult. For all of the dreaming and planning that the original group did, there was now a household full of new mem-bers who had their own dreams, opinions, and hopes for what the community could be. The new board pulled back from its involve-ment in the day-to-day life of the Lucy Stone Cooperative and shifted its focus to institutional development and administration, and the housemates began to coalesce around norms and cultures of living together.

The planning team had begun with a vision of Beloved Community—a community that welcomed adults, families, elders, and animals, with a diversity of ages, abilities, and racial and cultural backgrounds. Our reality has, at times, been filled with our own needs, fears, allergies, and limitations on energy, time, and space. The distance between our vision and our reality has oscillated between serving as a source of motivation for personal and organizational growth and a source of sadness and discour-agement when the community does not live up to our vision of Beloved Community.

The first few years of UUCC and the Lucy Stone Coopera-tive were full of sacred moments, unexpected hilarity, and some intense and humbling growing pains. We had conflict around shared space, vision, and values, and how to best put shared values into practice. Some original housemates chose to move out when it became clear that the culture that was developing was not going to work for them. The separation of UUCC and the cooperative involved letting go of some of the hopes and dreams the founders had, as the Lucy Stone Cooperative widened its community and included more voices and visions in its continuous creation.

One of the limitations of the Lucy Stone Cooperative is that while we believe in abundance when communities join together, we do have an actual limitation regarding the number of people we can fit in a single house. When a room becomes available, we have often felt pressed to choose the one "right candidate," sometimes feeling like identities or personal qualities of candidates are pitted against each other. In reality, most of the people who apply to live at the Lucy Stone Cooperative would bring so much to, and would flourish living in, intentional faith-based community. In the first three years of the Lucy Stone Cooperative's existence, we had over sixty people apply for the five rooms that became available for permanent housemates, leaving us confident of the need and desire for more communities like the Lucy Stone Cooperative.

A little over a year after the Lucy Stone Cooperative housemates moved in, we decided that we needed to think about the future of the organization. We participated in a day-long strategic planning meeting with our membership, board, and community members. Coming out of that meeting, we wrote a new organizational mission statement for UUCC: "Grounded in the values and tradition of Unitarian Universalism, Unitarian Universalist Community Cooperatives grows intentional housing communities of spiritual practice, sustainability, and social change."

We also wrote a document outlining our shared theological grounding and set five-year goals. The most prominent outcome of our strategic planning was that it highlighted our interest in acquiring more than one property—to expand the model that the Lucy Stone Cooperative has proven was successful. The other five-year goals that we developed included branding and communications strategies; documentation procedures; spiritual nourishment and developing our religious identity; widening our partners, networks, and extended community; financial development; skill building and innovation; clarifying our governance structure; and doing work around diversity, antiracism, anti-oppression, and multiculturalism.

We felt a call to expand our model so that the availability of intentional, faith-based living communities could grow. In March, 2015, we began our real estate search for our second house, the Margaret Moseley Cooperative. We pulled together a core team of future housemates who worked with UUCC's board to set the vision and priorities for this house, which will share our core values of spiritual practice, sustainability, and social change. At the time of this writing, we have just completed the purchase of this house, located less than a mile from the Lucy Stone Cooperative.

Living Our Unitarian Universalist Values and Tradition

We believe that Unitarian Universalism can and should be a relevant, transformative religion in our larger world. By honoring where we have come from and recognizing that we are a part of something larger than ourselves, we connect ourselves to rituals, ancestors, and histories that support us in times of need and inspire our work today.

Yet what does it actually mean to be a housing cooperative based in the values and traditions of Unitarian Universalism? What does it mean to live the Unitarian Universalist faith seven days a week? What makes a UU cooperative different from a secular or another faith cooperative? These difficult questions spawn answers as diverse as answers to the question "What is Unitarian Universalism?"

Our commitment to our core values of sustainability, spiritual practice, and social change has been a grounding force in the life of our community. When we look to make decisions as a community, we continually go back to our core values and assess whether our opinions are based on personal preference or whether they bring us more in line with our collective values and goals, pulling us closer to being the community and the individuals that we want to be, even when it isn't always comfortable.

Because we are a spiritually and religiously based community, practices like sharing a reading or a breath together for grace before dinner and lighting a chalice at the beginning of our house meetings are usual for us. Our regular Sunday evening singing is a touchstone in the week for many—residents and community members alike—while other housemates regularly meet to meditate. We know that individual and shared spiritual growth contributes to the larger whole. Some of our most profound moments have been in times of struggle when we have leaned on spiritual practice to support our community. We value the ineffable, the sacredness of relationship, the awe and the magic that happens when people come together. We recognize that we are a part of something larger than ourselves when we cook and pack lunches for each other or attend wider community meetings in our neighborhood on behalf of the cooperative.

We live our values better by living in community. We are nourished, supported, challenged, held, and loved in community. Through cooperative ownership and cooperative living, we reflect our belief that we are interconnected in more ways than we can know. When we come together in cooperation and intentional community, we nurture those fragile, life-sustaining strands of the web that weave our lives together.

Covenanting with Our Larger Faith

Our relationship to Unitarian Universalism has also been one of the complex and evolving aspects of the organization and the community's identity. We say that we are "grounded in the values and tradition of Unitarian Universalism," but what that means can be interpreted in a number of ways—through the identities of individuals in the community, through our practices and rituals, and though our values and our covenants.

We know that we are deeply relational beings and we gather in community to share our life's journeys. We believe that love is at the center of that journey. Like Unitarian Universalism, cooperative community is based in shared agreements of how we are in relationship. And covenant is the tool we use to be in intentional relationship, both interpersonally and institutionally with our wider faith. UUCC and the Lucy Stone Cooperative are both connected to larger Unitarian Universalism in both formal and informal covenantal relationships, as are many, though not all, of the members of UUCC.

As a non-congregational Unitarian Universalist community, we have often wrestled with what it means for us to be a community that is "grounded in the values and tradition of Unitarian Universalism" but doesn't require all of its members to identify as UU. Much like a congregation that does not require its members to identify as Unitarian Universalists but invites them to walk together in a shared journey, we too have a UU identity as an institution and our members, who have a diversity of paths and identities, have chosen to covenant together to live our shared values.

Unitarian Universalist identities weave throughout our entire house, as our faith nourishes our community and our community nourishes our faith. UU religious leaders serve on our board and live in the house. The backbone of our financing comes from the generosity of spirit and pocketbook of Unitarian Universalists. UU youth groups regularly stop by the Lucy Stone Cooperative on pilgrimage trips to Boston to join their voices in song and share their answers to one of our favorite questions, "How do we know that we're Unitarian Universalist, not just on Sundays when we're at church, but seven days a week?"

A faith that is as theologically diverse as Unitarian Universalism needs forms that reflect that diversity—and it seems that we have long been stuck in the fairly narrow form of the congregation. As a non-congregational UU organization, this has raised many questions about our place within Unitarian Universalism and its polity.

The Unitarian Universalist Association is an association of congregations, and yet we are not a congregation. We have pushed our denomination to think more expansively and our UUA has reciprocated by exploring what a covenantal relationship with UU communities beyond congregations might look like. As the denominational conversation about Congregations and Beyond and emerging ministries has begun to expand, we have found ourselves with a seat at the table for conversations about our denomination's polity and future in this realm. We have been part of the process of creating the new category of Covenanting Communities and were among the first groups that were recognized as such at General Assembly in 2015.

As a community straddling the line between the cooperative movement and Unitarian Universalism, we also see ourselves in a position to push each of those communities to integrate the best that the other has to offer: for Unitarian Universalism to be more cooperatively oriented in its culture and economics, and for cooperatives to be more spiritually grounded.

Lucy Stone resident Heather Concannon says of her own experience with UUCC,

> As someone who was raised UU, I've often longed for deeper ways to live out my faith. Living in an intentional community based in Unitarian Universalism has given me that opportunity to really wrestle with what my faith looks like in practice. It has challenged me to imagine a Unitarian Universalism that is deep, challenging, and spirit-filled—a Unitarian Universalism that takes risks and practices the hard and beautiful and sacred work of living in community, day in and day out.

Former Lucy Stone Cooperative housemate Barbara Seidl says this,

> Before living in community, I would go to events and see friends. After living in community, I go to events and see

community. I see people who share my beliefs and commitments, who are willing to work hard, to have difficult conversations, to keep showing up. I've lost track of the number of times I've gone alone to a rally, a training, a court date, a hearing, a community meeting and looked up to catch the eyes of up to a dozen former housemates in the crowd. It is a feeling of love, solidarity, security, faith, hope, and deep knowing that I haven't experienced in any other part of my life. Living in community means I have moved from knowing I'm not alone because there are people who love me to knowing I'm not alone in the ways I love the world.

We know that the world contains profound hurt, suffering, and brokenness on an individual and societal level. Because our human actions have profound effects on our world, we are called to be agents of healing through acts of justice, solidarity, compassion, and witness. We have faith and hope that a better world is possible, and we choose to live into that faith by building intentional community.

Although it is not new, much of what we are doing at the Lucy Stone Cooperative is unusual. We are offering Unitarian Universalists an alternative for where they can invest their money, in a way that aligns with their values. Through creating alternative structures of community-controlled home ownership, we are challenging the capitalist economic system that promotes self-sufficiency, individualism, and unchecked consumption. We know that our faith calls us to recognize our interdependence in both our theology, our planet, and our social structures, and we are exploring what it means to live out Unitarian Universalism every day of the week. We are working to articulate our practical, day-to-day theology of what it means to share living space and share this beautiful and aching world with one another and how we make meaning in that. We are sharing spiritual practices with one another, holding one another accountable to being our best selves, and learning from and growing with one another in community.

Our hope for Unitarian Universalism is that over time, non-congregational organizations like UUCC will become increasingly common and that we will take risks on behalf of our faith and find more opportunities to deeply engage with our faith. What if there was an approach to live our daily lives in ways that fully resonate with or are an extension of our faith tradition and values? What if we had communities and ways of engaging with our Unitarian Universalist values that were not limited to a singular form or a single day of the week, and were spiritually fulfilling and challenging?

We believe that these new models and expressions of Unitarian Universalism will allow us to deepen our theology and better understand what is truly at the center of our faith. We hope that Unitarian Universalism allows itself to imagine that which has never been done before, to not let professionalism get in the way of amateur dreaming, and to not let perfection get in the way of good. We hope that the model UUCC offers will allow all of us to think about using our resources and abundance to make radical changes in our own lives, in a journey toward a more whole, just, and loving world.

*Visit **www.uucommunitycoops.org**
to find out more about this organization*

Sanctuary Futures

DAVID RUFFIN

The Sanctuary Boston is a spiritual community of worship and connection, grounded in Unitarian Universalism, where seekers from all backgrounds and beliefs come together to find and co-create sanctuary. It is intentionally multigenerational, with ministry by and for young adults as a core but not a comprehensive value. We serve a diverse array of individuals nourished by spirit-filled, heart-centered worship and a community life built around opportunities for authentic connection and growth. At Sanctuary Boston, the power of music, deep sharing, and multivocal reflection renew our hearts and hold us together in love. We strive to create a place where our sorrows and joys can be expressed and held in their fullness, where we don't just affirm each individual's worthiness but each person feels holy and loved. This experience of love beyond belief calls us to build Beloved Community beyond the walls of any building.

This is not *the* story of the Sanctuary Boston but *a* story of the Sanctuary Boston. I tell it as Sanctuary's founder but, even for me, it's just one version of a tale that's consistently being revealed anew.

"Aha"

I was sitting in a park near my home on a gorgeous early summer afternoon, trying to step away from the pressures and stress of the day, when the serene scene of a young boy and his father caught my eye. The boy had a stick and was digging dirt, exploring beneath the tall grass. The man was reclining in the grass with his feet stretched out, his shoulders back, and his head tilted toward the sky (one eye, presumably, still on the little guy). As the young boy passed within his father's reach, he scooped up the child in a spontaneous, completely unrestrained embrace and began nuzzling him in the chest with abandon. The boy threw his head back and giggled with glee, arms dangling beneath him, soaking up the unexpected shower of affection. I, too, was surprised into laughter.

I remember reflecting that, at least as far as I could see, the boy had not done anything particularly remarkable to inspire this sudden display of affection. He hadn't dug his dirt more deftly than average. Rather, this was a parent's natural response to his child's being.

I felt my eyes get full. It was one of those moments when something you believe in, or want to believe in, hits you anew, right in your heart.

I thought, *Yeah. That's how much. That's how much I'm loved. No prereqs. That's how unrestrainedly, enthusiastically, playfully, spontaneously, fully I and each and every one of us are loved.* By whom-what-how-why can remain a marvelous mystery, but love's embrace reaching out for *all*, I felt that truth throughout my body.

And then, almost in the same moment, another thought arose: *That's also how much love I have* within *me.* That's how much care, compassion, consideration, creativity, affection, affirmation, appreciation, *love* are within me and each and every one of us, waiting to pour forth freely, liberated from the crippling restraints we've internalized and externalized—a natural response to the gift of life shared.

That's the truth we're here to realize in our living.

That's the "good news" experience we're called to receive and to share.

Of course, deeply experiential connection with this kind of foundational unconditional love is not often the norm day to day. Not for most of us. Certainly not for me. So we're often left trying to figure out how to respond to the apparent absence of an embrace we feel made for. And one way or another, we take on the burden of trying to fill that void. I know for me, no matter how many times poet Mary Oliver proclaims, "You do not have to be good!" and I say "Amen! Preach it, Mary," I fall back into striving to earn this, apparently missing, freely and fully given love.

That striving is a natural survival response in a world of disconnection. And it *is* often wrapped up in sincere efforts to do good, to do what I and others believe is right—even to bring justice! Yet without love's foundation we easily can slip into anxiety that actually restrains our hearts. Deep down we know that proving inherent worth and earning unconditional love are impossible tasks.

Yet while the need to earn this love may be an illusion, the pain of the gap between our need and our lived experience is real. We don't need this explained, we've all felt it. In a thousand ways on a thousand days we've found ourselves somehow alone again on the playground. And we've all found ways to try and numb our deep longing because of this pain, be it work or shopping or success or Facebook or Netflix or drugs or sex or drink or gambling or food. And many of us have, at times, lost hope for love at all, slipping into dark depressions.

However manifest, we know that failing to experience the deeper reality of love's embrace is nothing short of crippling to the spirit and, of course, our relationships with one another.

On the flip side, we know that finding ways to surface, experience, and share this deeper reality of unconditional universal love is holy, life-saving work.

Embraced by Religious Community

In early 2005, after seven years away from the Christian church of my upbringing, I walked into a Unitarian Universalist church for the first time. I remember saying I was looking for community to support my spiritual seeking. True, but I was hurting. I'd been struggling with depression, swimming in deep confusion

around vocation, identity, and self-worth. I felt painfully disconnected and unsure of love's embrace. Whether or not I had the
words to describe it, I longed to reconnect to a deeper reality of
love. I longed to be re-bound ("religio-ed") to . . . God? The spirit?
Humanity? All the above?

After years away, something led me to place new hope in a
church that morning.

And, I got lucky. During worship, out of powerful spoken
prayer and sacred shared silence, the voices of the congregation
rose together, seemingly spontaneously, enveloping me in the
warm presence of their prayerful song. I found myself joining my
voice to theirs, singing, "Spirit of Life come unto me, . . . hold me
close . . . set me free"—and then *feeling* it—feeling love actually
come and embrace me, throughout my mind, body, and soul. I was
broken, yes, but I was not alone in my pain. I was held in love. I
was part of this love. I was whole.

I cried tears of healing release. And, as can happen when the
spirit moves, tearful release soon opened my heart to thanksgiving
and celebration. "Hallelujah!" was not an exclamation I expected
my lips to form that morning, but they did, along with handclaps,
singing, and dancing. Because that's how love works, I've found. It
needs our contribution. It calls us into the joy of its sharing.

As I left that worship service and went back to my weekly rou-
tine, my challenges had not been resolved, of course, but love was
flowing far more freely in and out of me. I didn't miss a service for
months.

My Journey to the Sanctuary

But why do I say I got lucky?

Though this palpable embrace was my first impression of Unitarian Universalism, I came to realize that it was an uncommon
experience. As I toured across the country working as an actor, I
visited many Unitarian Universalist communities. In congregation
after congregation I heard inspiring messages, met lovely people,

and generally felt warmly welcomed. But I rarely experienced the
kind of spiritual embrace that had helped open my heart anew—
an embrace that brought me from the world of the "spiritual but
not religious" back into community. The need for and expression
of love were still present in these communities, as they were in
me, of course. Most communities I encountered named this reality
clearly and beautifully. But the spirit of love's invitation, presence,
expression, and celebration felt somehow restrained, like a father's
pat on my back when what I deeply needed was a bear hug. It was
almost as if church simply wasn't envisioned as the time or place
to experience that.

However, the hope I found in these communities still supported my faith. In fact, to my surprise, a sense of call to ministry
eventually took me to Harvard Divinity School. But my searching
for a church home that wouldn't hold back on me continued. I also
longed to share religious community with others closer to my age.

Beyond the Unitarian Universalist umbrella, I discovered
much of what I sought in a small emergent Christian community
and a local black Baptist church—both offering more embodied
worships with engaging music, ritual, and prayer. Still, Christian
community didn't feel like a home either. How incongruous it
seemed to me that in the cradle of Unitarian Universalism and a
city teeming with young adults, I couldn't find fulfilling worship.

Maybe others shared my longing? I wondered. I began asking
that question a lot, and found many who did, many who wanted to
actually feel the higher love they believed in. And some who even
shared my conviction that we should be able to experience this in
church (of all places).

Contemporary religious writers describe the postmodern
landscape as revealing a shift from a modern, individualistic
emphasis on belief to an emphasis on experience, feeling, and
community. When this new emphasis is not being expressed in
the religious sphere (such as mainline churches), religious decline
accelerates. On the other hand, when an emphasis on spiritual
experience *is* embraced, new vitality returns to religion.

I realized that though Unitarian Universalists should be in the forefront of this kind of change, we are far from it. We're often stuck in our heads, although mostly about what we don't believe. We aren't "corpse cold," however, as Ralph Waldo Emerson once chastened Harvard Divinity seminarians. I'd seen and felt the warmth of Unitarian Universalists time and again.

So maybe rather than running, I needed to trust just a little more. Maybe many souls like me were just waiting for yet uptapped love-beyond-belief power to be released in new forms. Maybe those of us yearning for such worship and community experiences could follow our hearts and start digging for the water we thirsted for. Maybe I could trust in love enough to believe my need for it would be met, if I was willing to surrender to it and *leap*.

My conversations with other seminarians quickly evolved into creative work, and the Sanctuary Boston began to take shape. First Church in Boston and First Parish in Cambridge agreed to back its creation, with gatherings alternately hosted by these two churches. We sought and gratefully received seed funding from the Fund for Unitarian Universalism and the Massachusetts Bay District. Leaders for the music we dreamed of came on board in drummer Matt Meyer and music director Mark David Buckles. And in May 2012 a team came together with butcher-block paper, hope, and a lot of heart to begin the work of bringing a community to life.

Envisioning Sanctuary

The effort to start not just a new form of worship but a new spiritual community was a brazen move for a group of seminarians. Yet, despite strong church partnerships, we weren't envisioning just a new form of worship for existing communities. We wanted to create a space of connection and trust between our two church locations. We also believed our worship gatherings would attract many who were not currently churchgoers and who might not, at least immediately, feel they could call these churches home. This led us to *ground* our community in Unitarian Universalism rather than *identify* as a UU community. We sensed new possibilities for welcome with an even broader spiritual-religious embrace.

And building community was in fact the key learning passed on to us from prior efforts to create alternative Unitarian Universalist forms of worship. For example, Rev. Marlin Lavanhar and his wife Anitra created Soulful Sundowns at First Church in Boston a decade earlier. These were alternative monthly worship services that had drawn hundreds, largely young adults. They were successful in Boston and also in inspiring the creation of Soulful Sundown services across the country. Lavanhar cautioned that Soulful Sundowns lacked the capacity to nurture community among attendees, negatively affecting the project's longevity and depth. With such guidance confirming our conviction, we took a deep breath and set off to build a community.

Creating the kind of worship that we yearned for and sensed others needed was also a clear priority. It's remarkable how closely what we were able to realize mirrors what we had envisioned. I say this not to lift up our vision as particularly on point but as testimony that with commitment and passion visions can be brought to life.

We began where probably anyone creating worship should begin: by lifting up past worship or worshipful experiences that had been meaningful, ones that had moved, inspired, renewed, held, shaped, and transformed us—and exploring why. I shared my story of my first Unitarian Universalist worship, my memories of the mystery of Christmas Eves with candlelit "Silent Nights," of the fuller engagement of my heart and body that I'd felt in emergent Christian community and black church contexts. Others spoke of UU revivals they'd held at the Unitarian Universalist Urban Ministry, of worship with Boston Unitarian Universalist Young Adults (another prior alternative worship), of Harvard Unitarian Universalist Ministry for Students worship, of Sunday evening sings around the table at the Lucy Stone Cooperative, of enthusiastic Shabbat services in another local Jewish co-op, of experiences worshipping in UU youth conferences, and so on. We spoke of concerts, festivals, theater, coffeehouses, and poetry slams, and of embodied experiences like dance, yoga, and meditation. We lifted up the power of ritual and spoke of the intimacy, authenticity, and power of small group ministry.

From these stories the core building blocks of our worship vision became clear:

Experiential Worship engages the whole person, body, mind, heart, soul.

Worship as a practice Worship is something we actively *do* together to transform ourselves individually and collectively; a practice, not a product.

Spirit-filled, enthusiastic Worship fills worshippers with the spirit of love; whether through gospel praise music or meditation, it's safe to surrender to such love.

Heart-centered Worship provides less information for the head and more space for connection, vulnerability.

Music that moves Music we *love* and that *feels* integrated throughout worship as well as our lives—that is, it also feeds and sustains us outside church.

Multivocal Worship is co-creative and connective; practice not product.

Ritualistic Sacred space is made for spiritually transformative community ritual.

Flowing Worship flows in an emotional arc without unnatural interruption.

Intentional and informal Worship is carefully crafted but accessible; it honors the fact that a less formal atmosphere has a natural draw for many.

A key question that emerged early on was about our use of language of reverence. We had to grapple with the age-old Unitarian Universalist conundrum about what theology would hold this community together, especially when trying to get beyond the judicious restraint that characterizes much of UU worship.

I originally imagined that theistic rather than humanistic theological framings and language would best support the spirit-filled worship we envisioned. As one who found Unitarian Universalism later in life, I felt indebted to the way this faith values rational free will, because it had freed me from obstructive dogma. But in my longing for an experience of transformative connection with a love beyond my comprehension, I often encountered UU worship that felt imprisoned by rationalism. I began to lament the strong humanist presence in our tradition. Pointing a finger, I suggested "they"—the humanists—threw the baby out with the bathwater.

But even in my small team of collaborators committed to spirit-filled worship, there was significant theological diversity. Some resonated with God language, others did not. I had never thought to vet my collaborators on theological conformity! In this way, we were as Unitarian Universalist as could be. And yet we'd gathered with a common longing. And in practice it became clear we could share powerful spiritual experiences beyond naming. If a baby had been all but lost with the bath water, I realized it was this heartfelt experiential connection, not any specific understanding of it. So while surprised by the diversity of our ideas, I felt empowered by our team's early faith that love—experienced, not just asserted—would hold us together. This kept our eyes on the prize.

It still took almost two years before I felt I could confidently articulate our shared experiential grounding in a way that would resonate across our diversity. Once we were living it, however, it was decidedly easier to find words that pointed toward our shared experience.

The experience, the practice, the theological grounding of Sanctuary Boston is embrace itself. If we had a warning label, it would read, "You will be hugged on this ride" (though we try to practice consent-based hugging).

Our worship, as indeed all of our community life, is crafted to help co-create the shared experience of embrace. When we sing (and sing and sing) together, as in the lyrics from our theme song "Sanctuary"—"Make us aware we are a Sanctuary, each made holy, and loved right through"—we reach beyond affirmations of inherent worth and love for all toward a personal and shared experience of those realities. When we repeat a chorus or phrase two or three (or ten!) times, it allows that experience to be experienced in its fullness. When we light candles symbolizing our own light and pass the flame between us, pausing to see each other, we feel it again. When we open a space for vulnerability by honestly sharing the burdens we're carrying, we feel our own need. When we receive and respond to each person's sharing, singing "Walking with you is our prayer," we feel our capacity to meet that need. When we let it all hang out, shaking out our bodies, clapping, stomping, or raising our hands, we co-create a celebration we feel born for and without which something within withers. When we hold hands, physically connecting, and pray aloud beyond our knowing and understanding, we open to the experience of embrace in another way.

We've found that by reaching with expectancy, really opening to love, the experience becomes more available. This higher love can indeed be felt "right through."

We strive to fill worship with inspired personal reflection, including learning and tools to guide and support our meaning making and spiritual growth. We share this work among us. The power and depth of the messages we lift up and grapple with comes from being grounded in stories from our hearts, giving diverse gifts of insight but also of vulnerability, authenticity, beauty, strength, and love.

At Sanctuary, we trust that with each person bringing one's sacred *whole* self, each a sanctuary, to the community, we can co-create the living, loving sanctuary we all so deeply need. Through experiencing this sanctuary together, we can shake off the illusion and burden of disconnection and be caught up anew in the sacred embrace of love beyond belief.

We don't know where the universal circle of love that we celebrate begins. We do know that we have both great need for that love and great capacity to co-creatively realize it anew, every time we gather. And so, embraced, embracers, embracing, we keep singing.

Make us aware we are a Sanctuary
Each made holy, and loved right through.
With thanksgiving, we are a living Sanctuary . . . anew.

Stories of Sanctuary's Embrace

A glimpse of the larger Sanctuary story calls for the voices of those who are co-creating the experience in the actual living, growing, ever-evolving community that's given meaning to our name. By the time this book is published I won't even have been directly involved in Sanctuary's co-creation for more than a year! The stories that could be told here are as numerous as the individuals within the community. Here are just a few windows into the Sanctuary community:

Being steeped in my form of Christian tradition, I sometimes am amazed when I find myself in a different worship setting. When I came to the Sanctuary—I can't lie—I remember I was somewhat wary. But then I remember it came to a portion of time devoted to group prayer. A person would share their joy or their woe, and we all would sing, "Walking with you, walking with you is our prayer." And in that moment I felt it didn't matter what I believed or who I was, but that I was walking with these people. I felt deeply connected to people who sat next to me, in front and behind me, that I'd never met. Raising our voices in prayer united us in ways that I feel many of us are deeply desiring but so often missing in our lives.

More personally, I had suffered a bout of depression not too long before walking into the Sanctuary during which I felt very disconnected. I had already begun to connect before walking into the Sanctuary, but I don't think it was until I was singing those words that I realized how reconnected to people I was. It allowed me to walk out of worship and carry that connection around with me to every place I went.

—Patrick Kangrga

It's difficult for me to verbalize how deeply the Sanctuary has touched my life. The past couple of years have been extremely difficult for me. My father was very ill, my parents got divorced, my best friend, Ryan, and my grandmother both passed away, then another friend was killed in a car accident, and my mother was diagnosed with breast cancer. Yeah. Through all of this, worship at the Sanctuary simply spoke to my soul—I can't think of any other way to put it. While I was experiencing some of the worst days of my life, I was renewed and held and felt able to face another day through the love and support of the Sanctuary—both at worship and through the community in general.

I have never felt closer to the sacred, the divine mystery, whatever it is that you can feel within your soul but can't explain, than during worship with the Sanctuary. When thinking about loving energy, or the sacred, in the past most of my experiences of feeling held and surrounded by love were very personal and solitary. Times when, for example, I was surrounded by nature and observed the most perfectly formed flower, or when reading and I was transported into a different reality where I could escape and be free, or when I've turned my music up as loud as it could possibly go and sang and danced around my room (with no one watching!). Those are the times I've felt most connected, and most loved or loving—times I could feel the energy of something larger than myself.

And then I found the Sanctuary. I found a community where I could just show up, as myself, with all of my brokenness and imperfection, and I was embraced and held; where I could open my heart without fear of judgment or ridicule. And I found in that space a deeper sense of connection and love than I had ever felt by myself. Just being surrounded by people, who also weren't perfect (or even close to it), who were willing to come together to try to be open and loving to all who came through the door, who were willing to experiment with lowering the walls around all of us that we construct. It's incredibly difficult to translate an experience like this to paper. I don't think any words I can come up with do it justice. I guess it all just comes back to love. I've felt more loved and whole while worshipping with the Sanctuary than I ever have before. I've truly been held by this community.

—Lauren Robinson

Somehow I had managed to spend my entire life as a Unitarian Universalist (and enter seminary) believing strongly in affirming and promoting the inherent worth and dignity of every person, and still did not know what to do when my own inherent worth and dignity were being attacked. I was pretty good at taking care of other people. I was equally pretty awful at taking care of myself. That began to change when I showed up at Sanctuary. I remember sitting there when we sang our adaptation of the Sanctuary song and lighting my candle and sensing, "Hey, now, maybe this 'we' can include me. Maybe I can be a sanctuary too. And maybe that means that I deserve better than what is happening to me right now." I carried that feeling around with me for a few days and eventually made the decision to make some pretty major changes in my life, including ending an unhealthy relationship and moving to Boston to fully focus on my studies and become more involved in Sanctuary.

A couple of months later we were doing a service that ended with the song "This Is the New Year" by A Great Big World. The last line of the chorus of the song says, "I will give the world to you." When Dave introduced the song, he told all of us to imagine our childhood self when we sing that line and imagine that we are giving the world to that child. So I did—I pictured my child-hood self, still within me, accepting the world from me. And I felt healed. I didn't walk away feeling that all my troubles had suddenly vanished, but I did end up becoming more aware of the part of myself that has always been and will always be hopeful and full of joy. Having become a Sanctuary leader, I'm now able to work with other people to help build and hold this community. But sharing this ministry with so many, it still remains a core space of love and healing for me.

   —Sam Teitel

Our family is a demographic outlier at the Sanctuary Boston: Two of us are solidly middle-aged and the third is just twelve. Our primary church home is at the Unitarian Universalist Church of Medford, a traditional New England congregation whose blended roots stretch back to both the Puritans and the first generations of Universalists. For us, the Medford church offers the experience of unconditional embrace and at-home-ness that many UU young adults have struggled to find at traditional congregations. But we are also committed to the Sanctuary Boston because we experience it as a whole-body, emotionally connected worship that complements our Sunday experience. At the Sanctuary, we sing and sing and sing until our bodies and spirits are in a new place. Significantly, all three of us share the entire worship experience together, rather than separating out into an adult sermon and children's religious education. We are able to bond as a family, while our daughter is mentored and nurtured by young adults who value her participation. We are thrilled to share this experiment with a large cohort of future UU ministers, as well as many young adults who've never participated in a UU congregation before. This gives us hope that the Unitarian Universalism of the future will offer a welcoming embrace to an ever-wider circle of people.

   —Tammy McKanan

Whether it's at table over a meal or in worship, it blows my mind sometimes just how much we each bring to any gathering. Our hearts, minds, and souls are filled with each and every thing we have ever lost, gained, hoped for, and dreamed about. While all of those things help make us who we are, there's something more to gathering time than who we are and what we bring as individuals.

It's who we can become, together, that's so precious. It's the space between us, that energy that brings me to you and you to me that has the power to bring Beloved Community to the surface.

When I first encountered the Sanctuary Boston community in October 2012, I didn't know if I could trust it. Like so many communities of faith before it, I wanted to know there was a way in, a way for me to fully show up as myself, a way for me to pull back all the layers of me and be vulnerable, a way for more love. As a queer- and trans-identified person of African descent, who also happens to be a person of faith, and who was also reeling from the death of my father, I didn't just want a way in—I desperately needed it! I needed it in a way I didn't even have words for.

So when I showed up, only weeks before my ordination and in deep pain over the fact that my dad wouldn't be with me at such a special time, I honestly wasn't sure what to expect, what I'd be able to let go of, or what I'd manage to leave with. But something truly marvelous happened. The arms of a community showed up and wrapped themselves around me. The music of a community showed up and laid the tune of possibility inside me. The love of a community showed up and offered me and all that I carried a place to sit down, settle in, and be healed; so I could leave with some hopefulness that I couldn't see when I entered, so that the embrace I'd lost sight of could be reclaimed.

—Rev. Mykal Slack

Key Learnings for Entrepreneurial Ministry

Mykal, the author of the last story, became director of worship after my departure. Sanctuary was newly blessed by Mykal's ministry, as by the leadership of others who continue serving.

But how did we arrive at the point where, within two years of the community's founding, we were able to transition leadership and continue growing into our vision, while also growing practically as a community and organization? "Give us the play by play!" some have asked. It has been a journey with *so* much learning, with many highs and lows. We could never have created what we created without each other. We've also sometimes felt that we could never create this *with* each other! That contradiction is, of course, well known in any community.

Although we ultimately charted some uncharted waters in this work, it has not been with particular expertise or ease. In truth, while the work has been joyful, it also has been very hard. The behind-the-scenes stories deserve to be shared, but many of them are also tender tales with many valuable perspectives beyond my own.

With grand visions, I've learned, so also comes grand disillusionment. My main regret is that I wasn't more accepting of the times when the reality of our efforts didn't match our vision—both for myself and for others. Thankfully, beneath disillusionment, love abides.

Still, I'd like to share some of our specific learnings, hoping they can be useful to individuals, congregations, and others considering alternative worship and/or community models, as well as to the larger faith community as it considers how to support such efforts.

My experience with the Sanctuary Boston has demonstrated that *entrepreneurial ministry*, as many new frontier ministries are being called, requires significant investment. Much of the investment can and should be in training and leadership development, such as in business planning and leadership for start-ups. The more that such training can happen in seminary the better, but other options for serious, UU-based training are key. The Unitarian Universalist Ministers Association is taking the lead here, but congregations also need to get in on this. And even with that training, creative entrepreneurs need to be well resourced while in action. We can't do this without help.

Entrepreneurial outreach ministries as programs of existing congregations have advantages within our congregational organizational structure; they are a growing phenomenon and should be encouraged. They also have drawbacks, the most obvious ones being the inclination for congregations to prioritize existing services and members and the challenge of empowering new leaders bringing fresh ideas.

Entrepreneurial ministries that are not fully resourced programs of existing congregations may have more innovative freedom. Yet they will likely struggle to develop and to become sustainable without strong support from another locus. Considering our Unitarian Universalist denominational polity, this is a major adaptive challenge. That said, while I imagine "congregations" *will look different*, far more than Sanctuary does for that matter, I'm a traditionalist in my belief that we should maintain our focus on building and nurturing community. I believe it will always be the heart of who we are.

So, to the brave souls called to this work of new community building or church planting, here is a list of top ten lessons learned from our successes and failures alike:

1. Before beginning, know who you are as a person. Know what you're about at your core, and know who you feel called to serve. Hold on to this grounding vision. It's your call into the ministry of realizing your vision. But don't confuse the particulars of your vision with what calls your vision forth.

2. Don't give up your work or vision in the face of resistance. As Saul Alinsky said, "Change means movement. Movement means friction."[1] Not everyone will be supportive, certainly not as you hoped. Hold on to the truth of your call.

3. At the same time, be willing to be changed by what you've started. Any creative community venture is, by nature, collaborative. Along with this, expect some disillusionment of your dream! "Those who choose their dream of community over community itself, become destroyers of community, be their intentions ever so earnest."[2]

4. Build community, not just worship. And start this work before you go live. Focus exploratory time on the practices and experiences shared (worship, small groups, social gather-

---

1 Saul D. Alinsky, *Rules for Radicals: A Pragmatic Primer for Realistic Radicals* (New York: Random House, 1971), 21.
2 Adapted from Dietrich Bonhoeffer, *Life Together: The Classic Exploration of Christian in Community* (New York: HarperOne, 2009), p. 27.

ings, justice opportunities) and on the people and relationship building. Let the community grow from shared experience and connection. Let it grow from the spirit.

5. Don't officially launch until you're really ready to *keep* rolling. For starters, if you've followed step 4, then you have a community to launch your community. Even so, it's a marathon and once you're official, it doesn't stop. So plan ahead. Week two, three, and four, and on and on, come quickly on the tail of week one. Create sustainable systems for doing what you need to do so that you can direct your energy where it will have the greatest impact.

6. Once launched, resist the pressure you will feel (internally and externally) to be an "adult church," a grown-up organization. It's more than okay to let things develop organically. You will burn out if you try to grow into the fullness of your vision in your first months or even the first few years of the community's life. Build on what's core and take your time.

7. Entrust early-stage decision making with trustworthy individuals, but as few as possible. Against all Unitarian Universalist instinct, do *not* begin your efforts by forming a board of directors nor even doing so in the first two to three years. You need the energy of early invested leaders for community building and outreach. Rather than power through the democratic process, harness the power of relationship. Develop clear and honest communication and expectations, and, most of all, trust itself! If you're working with existing congregations or other organizations, also harness the power of their oversight and blessing.

8. Covenant early and often. Creating something new inevitably calls us into the messy terrain outside existing structures and the clarity of roles, relationships, and expectations those structures bring. You may find that a surprising amount of normal assumptions are not to be assumed. Whether among your team or with partner congregations, investors, or even future members, it is essential to create covenants that can hold you in the in-between spaces of creative ministry. What do we have if not each other?

9. Maintain your own daily spiritual practices and personal life and do not give them up. Really. It just doesn't work out well if you do.

10. Have fun! Make space for joy, especially with your core team, though don't stop there. As mentioned earlier, this is hard work, but it is also joyous. Give yourself and your community time to take in the wonder of what you've been called into. Soak up the gift of sharing the journey. Celebrate!

Now, to address the Unitarian Universalist world at large: Entrepreneurial ministries need us! Here are my top five ways to encourage UUA leadership to further support this transformative work:

1. Provide serious sustained financial investment, both centralized seed money and access to high-impact investors.

2. Provide devoted support (ideally, staffed personnel) for strategic and business planning, ongoing coaching, leadership training, information sharing between innovators, and so forth.

3. Provide guidance for handling decision making in the early stages of start-up ministries. When a community is in early development, the use of the community's scarce and highly demanded energy and time for the work of governance can be a hindrance to its growth. (for example, prior to development of community governance, when vision and community capacity are sufficiently developed to broaden such energy investment).

4. Be clear about expectations and accountability that come with these organizational and financial investments. This should include devoted supervision and mentorship, giving emerging leaders both critical feedback and appropriate cover in work that involves substantial risk.

5. Offer spiritual encouragement (with specific opportunities for entrepreneurs).

Finally, here are three big-picture goals to support more creative Unitarian Universalist ministry:

- To work toward a more missional culture centered on personal transformation and outreach beyond our walls and built upon greater trust in leadership

- To renew work to articulate this active shared mission of personal and public transformation grounded in love beyond belief, rather than emphasizing shared Principles

- To work toward a more supportive environment for creativity, risk, and failure—it's time to really receive the good news of Unitarian Universalism!

A Hopeful Beginning

Just as my version is only one story in Sanctuary's story, Sanctuary is just one story in a much larger story that all of us are a part of. Our calling is not to be a diet religion—a calorie-free version of something we determined we didn't need but still kind of liked. Those calories are our spiritual and emotional energy. They've just been misunderstood.

Our world is in deep need of a renewed sanctuary movement, because each and every life is clearly *not* seen as equally sacred. If people are to truly see each living being as a sanctuary, our precious earth included, and to behave accordingly, we must reconnect with the spiritual power of feeling that truth in our bodies and throughout our relationships. It's time to reclaim both our need for sanctuary and our power to co-create the living sanctuary of unconditional, universal love that embraces every life right through. Sanctuary Boston has experienced a hopeful beginning on this journey. We hope we can inspire others to follow their own hearts' leading. The more caught up we all become in the circle of love's embrace, the more freed we will become to be the change we so deeply wish to see.

*Visit **thesanctuaryboston.org***
to learn more about this community

AWAKE Ministries, Annapolis, Maryland

Turning Toward Wholeness

FREDRIC MUIR, JOHN T. CRESTWELL JR., AND CHRISTINA LEONE TRACY

The congregation we serve, the Unitarian Universalist Church of Annapolis (UUCA), has a long-standing goal of becoming a multicultural congregation. The Unitarian Universalist Association's website defines multiculturalism as "nurturing a religious community where people of all races, ethnicities and cultures see their cultural identities reflected in every aspect of congregational life—worship, fellowship, leadership, governance, religious education, social justice, etc." We would expand the definition by saying this: Multiculturalism is contextual. Multicultural identities will not be the same in every community, but every context is (or can be) multicultural. Therefore, multiculturalism is defined by a congregation's location; the same multicultural characteristics cannot exist in every congregation, but that doesn't mean a congregation or program can't be multicultural.

UUCA's intentional journey to a multicultural ministry began with the Journey Toward Wholeness (JTW) curriculum distributed at the 1997 UUA General Assembly, where the JTW Resolution passed nearly unanimously. This vote was the UUA's promise to address the challenges of racism, oppression, and multiculturalism in our congregations and programs. At UUCA one of ways the JTW resolution found expression is in AWAKE Ministries, one of the several ministries the congregation has embraced on its journey to becoming a multicultural, intergenerational faith community. AWAKE stands for: Actualize your Wisdom, Awaken to your Karma and Engage the process. AWAKE's "manfiesto" says: "AWAKE Ministries is a faith-based multicultural movement of human reconciliation that edifies the worth and dignity in all human beings by inspiring and empowering them to live bold and compassionate lives. We strategically partner with progressive congregations and community organizations through interfaith worship, emotional literacy workshops and classes, life-coaching, and consultations." AWAKE was born out of and flourishes because of a deep love for the congregation's Unitarian Universalist heritage and future, a future that is bright if we turn away from the "trinity of errors": individualism, exceptionalism, and our aversion to authority. These errors do not promote or support the multiculturalism that is rapidly becoming the norm in North American towns and cities. Consequently, Unitarian Universalists must change the way we do church.

This is a journey not of optimism but of hope. Optimists believe something will go the way they would like; they generally expect that things are going to turn out okay, with the desired outcome. Hope, however, is knowing something is moral and right, and working for it in spite of what others say. When we are hopeful we are willing to be involved. Optimism is passive; hope is active.

AWAKE is a ministry of hope. It is still incomplete; still emerging. It is a ministry shaped not by errors but by promises. It's a ministry that has moved the congregation from tipping point to turning point.

Anticipating the Tipping Point

A tipping point is that place where change, in one direction or another, becomes unstoppable, taking on a life of its own. Changing demographics, lifestyles, and religious preferences were bringing UUCA to a tipping point. We took a number of actions to anticipate it and to turn our future toward wholeness.

Our first action was to develop a plan to follow. Too often some believe that if we simply share our message, market our gospel to the right places, and get people into our building through events, then the result will be the community we desire. This approach is a kind of magical thinking. Of course these actions will contribute to the goal, but multiculturalism requires an intentional, step-by-step, deliberate plan that takes members and friends on the journey together. For UUCA, this meant partnering with others outside our congregation; we realized from the start that this was something we could not do alone. We turned to UUA staff who welcomed the opportunity to walk with us and share their learnings. Partnering includes an element of risk and humility, because individually and as a congregation you have to expose and reveal yourselves in the process; indeed, it is a necessary first step.

Our second step involved changing our governance. The congregation moved to a version of policy governance that empowered the professional ministers to make commitments and give direction to a vision named by the congregation and shaped by the board. The vision comes from members, the board shapes the vision into goals, and the ministry team implements the vision. Our vision—in governance jargon, "the Global Ends Statement"—states, "The Unitarian Universalist Church of Annapolis exists to create the Beloved Community by inspiring and empowering all souls to lead bold and compassionate lives."

Again, it's the ministry team's responsibility to carry out this vision; and just as the team is accountable to each other, we are also accountable to the board. It is not the board's role to manage the ministry that addresses the vision, but the ministry team must inform the board about what we are doing to realize the vision. Many ministers would find this style of governance liberating since it frees them to live the ministry to which they have been called.

Our third step involved moving from outreach to inreach. This is one of the most challenging shifts. Unitarian Universalists have a significant and impressive history of justice-making ministries in and with the larger community. To be clear, we are not suggesting that this history and the ongoing justice work be slowed or abandoned. However, sometimes we Unitarian Universalists would rather do our ministry with partners in the larger community than recognize the justice-making ministry that is needed in our own congregations. Doesn't it often look and feel easier to go out and partner and build coalitions with others in order to change the world than it is to shape our congregation into the Beloved Community as described in our Principles? Initiating and sustaining the journey to wholeness within a congregation may be as challenging—if not more so—as outside it. Efforts to change the world easily ignore—often conveniently and with the label of hypocrisy—the hard and humbling ministry to shape our own congregations as Beloved Communities. This is what we mean by moving from outreach to inreach: living the Purposes and Principles in our faith home.

Balancing was another critical action as we anticipated our tipping point. We needed to keep our eyes on the prize, knowing that there will be detours, stops, and starts, frustrations and disappointments as well as times of joy and celebration. We found that it helps to meditate, pray, sing, and look onward to the next milestone. We have to stay focused and balanced as a congregation, ministry team, and board, and remember that this is a journey for at least a generation. It took 250 to 300 years for Unitarian Universalist congregations to get where they are today; it will take more than a three- to five-year strategic plan to redirect a congregation.

An essential aspect of all our actions was flexibility. There are times when the plan isn't working and we have to reimagine and start over. With all the practice, planning, and good ideas, there will still be changes and redirection. But with each person sharing the experiences of partnering, learning, and ministry, insights and promise can abound!

Understanding the process as a spiritual journey was another way we prepared for our tipping point. We believe this is a spirituality composed of and built on a "trinity of promises." The first promise is generosity rather than individualism. Unitarian Universalism is a faith with a generous spirit. We are a liberal religion, which means to be open and embracing because we know that "revelation is not sealed." Let ours be a welcoming and open posture. Another promise: We welcome pluralism rather than exceptionalism. With pluralism comes an engagement with others premised on the desire and willingness to go deep with each other. And the third promise, which is imagination rather than rebellion. Imagination means thinking, seeing, and living beyond the present and into the future.

Intentionally creating multigenerational community was another way we anticipated our tipping point. Multiculturalism is the focus of AWAKE Ministries and age is a form of culture. People of different ages and stages of life are also in our surrounding communities, and so when we engage with them, we're doing so across a different culture.

Pete Seeger was a writer, singer, and activist, and a beloved Unitarian Universalist. After his death in 2014, we at UUCA, like many others, honored him during our Sunday service by singing "Hammer Song." During the time for all ages in our Sunday service we put a hammer in what we call our Wonder Box. We talked about the hammer, we sang that song, and it was fantastic! After the service someone came up to one of us, Christina Leone Tracy, and exclaimed, "Why don't we sing Pete Seeger every Sunday? Everybody knows and loves Pete Seeger's music—everybody!" Everybody knows the Pete Seeger songs?

Christina, who is thirty-two, didn't grow up with Pete Seeger; she knows only a couple of his songs. We can't assume that everybody knows and loves Pete Seeger; it's just not true. This is just an example, but congregations often make these same kinds of assumptions. We assume that we're all white or one political party or all above the age of fifty. We assume we are all living with the same experiences and information and know the same things and, therefore, everyone should. But it's just not true.

There are two ways to think about generation. One is age and stage, and the other is generation as cohort. With age and stage, there are youth—generally defined as fourteen to eighteen years old; young adults—eighteen to thirty-five; adults; and elders. Each stage has its own needs. Different developmental changes are occurring in the body and the brain, different things are happening in life—young children, new careers, retirement. Congregations need to take into consideration each generation and where a person is in that generation.

Generation as cohort refers to the Silent Generation, the Baby Boomers, the Gen Xers, and the Millennials. Much has been written on generational theory in recent years. We recommend *Generations* by Neil Howe and William Strauss and *Generations of Faith: A Congregational Atlas* by Carl Eeman. Eeman takes the work of Howe and Strauss and applies it to communities of faith. These authors say that a culture develops in generational cohorts. While saying, "All Boomers are like this" is just as false as saying, "All white people are like this," there are some commonalities in culture among a generational cohort that offer important information. For example, Boomers typically value consensus. Generation Xers generally believe action is important. So what that means in a meeting is that Boomers are going to want to talk a lot to make sure everybody is heard, while Generation Xers will want to make a decision and get going. Consequently, the Boomers might say to the Xers, "You're not being inclusive," and the Xers might say to the Boomers, "You're just talking and talking." These are different cultures, and they both have valid perspectives that needs to be worked out. Pluralism is about engaging in this conversation to hear each other, deepen relationships, and move forward together. Creating multigenerational community means honoring the gifts that each generation—each cohort, each age and stage—brings.

One way we do this at UUCA is with our Wonder Box. It looks like a small treasure chest. We invite a child to come up, open the box, and take out the object inside, and then we talk about it.[1] It's not only kids' time but a time when we engage all ages, speaking

---

1 Learn more about the Wonderbox at www.uua.org/re/multigenerational/ga/287054.shtml.

to children and adults at the same time. The animated movie company Pixar talks to all ages really well. Parents don't mind bringing their children to Pixar movies. If we can master Pixar moments in worship, we're doing well!

One of the things that we - the Annapolis Ministry Team with the Music Team - are excited about is how elements from AWAKE worship and Sunday morning worship support and highlight the other. With both we are creating Spirited Worship, which is multigenerational worship woven around a story and its themes. Rather than having a long story and a sermon that run the risk of boring children, youth, and adults, we break it up by weaving a narrative and/or its themes throughout the service. This means that there is not a sermon, but an ongoing narrative or theme-based story with parts of the liturgy woven into it. We are still experimenting with Spirited Worship; we've learned that there's no one right way to do it; we're just trying to be multigenerational and we stay with it, as does the congregation as we introduce and try new things.

Both AWAKE and traditional UUCA programming offer multigenerational events. It's likely that most congregations have events for all generations, but billing them as multigenerational is important. For example, the church's music director coordinates a cabaret, a night of singing and piano playing by everyone from little children to elders. We've also started a multigenerational dance called "Dancing on the Side of Love," where we do the dances of every generation: the hand jive and the hokey pokey, Gangnam Style and the wobble—all the songs so that everybody can take part in teaching and learning from each other.

Middle Hour is our religious exploration for children and youth, which is scheduled between the two services on Sunday rather than having it during one of the services, which was essentially saying to our youth that we didn't expect them to ever come to worship. Now we're saying, "We expect you will be part of the community during worship, but you still have your peer time." So now our worship can be truly multigenerational. We are asking our youth to be lay ministers, ushers, greeters, and chalice lighters.

The whole point of Middle Hour is to facilitate a truly multigenerational community rather than just saying that we are. The whole point of AWAKE Ministries is to bridge a wide range of cultures and ages.

The final action we took to set our direction and prepare for the tipping point was work to become an emotionally literate community. When we are emotionally literate we have the ability to articulate our emotions and underlying universal needs in positive ways that affirm the worth and dignity in ourselves and in others. This involves a paradigm shift, a reimagining of church. An emotionally literate society that lives Unitarian Universalist values makes the world a better place. Through AWAKE Ministries' worship services, workshops and classes, coaching, and consulting work, people from all backgrounds are helped to live into their true potential. AWAKE operates from the belief that

- when we achieve Beloved Community, it will be an emotionally literate and interculturally competent time, when humanity learns to live in balance and to manage aspirations and face fears in a healthy manner;

- when people practice compassion and empathy (the heart of emotional literacy) they do less harm in society;

- when people do less harm they are in harmony with what is best in themselves and others; their Christ or Buddha consciousness emerges.

The church's associate minister, John Crestwell, describes an "aha moment" when coming to grips with the content of emotional literacy:

I was the last person to think that I would be teaching and preaching about emotional literacy. During a painful divorce, I realized that, although I'm a minister, I really don't know how to communicate. A hard lesson resulted from that reality check: A lot of times your mess becomes your message, and I believe that my awakening to emotional literacy came as a result of not knowing how to communicate effectively my needs and emotions.

Emotional literacy was introduced to UUCA by a church member who had used this powerful and life-changing tool to shape our prison ministry at the Maryland Correctional Facility in Jessup, Maryland. This ministry was greatly diminished when the member moved away, a common experience in many church programs when the program founder and promoter moves on. So Christina and John partnered with others to re-establish the ministry. Emotional literacy then became the backbone of AWAKE, the spiritual, philosophical, and moral framework on which AWAKE Ministries was built.

In reading works by Robin Casarjian and Marshall Rosenberg (whose books UUCA uses in our prison ministry), we saw and experienced firsthand how emotional literacy was already a part of the church's ministry—we just hadn't labeled it. In naming it, we realized that emotional literacy was vital to our social justice ministries and to the life of the congregation—emotional literacy was vital to all of our ministries. As we continue to infuse the congregation and our programs with emotional literacy, it becomes an important part of the process, encouraging and leading us into a rich multicultural community life. Emotional literacy helps us understand the place from which we've come and the place to which we are going by deepening our core competency and strengthening our spiritual fiber.

As a ministry team we practice and live emotional literacy every day. We remind each other of our highest aspirations as we share the journey toward Beloved Community. We have no reason to believe that war, destruction, dogma, and fear are the means to take us there. It's much better to encourage people to find their personal freedom and to name their relationship to the God of their understanding. When people are in touch with their Creative Power, that Source, they arrive at a place of peace and clarity that may defy understanding. The Beloved Community is a place of love and trust in an environment of support and respect; it is a place of nonthreatening fairness and shared responsibility. Emotional literacy can take us there because it inspires and supports the church's mission statement: "The UUCA exists to create Beloved Community by empowering all souls to lead bold and compassionate lives," which can result when we reflect on and articulate our values and aspirations.

AWAKE Ministries is a justice-making, transforming ministry in a style and with a purpose unlike traditional Unitarian Universalist social justice ministries, which historically have been about leveraging power and education through partnering and using social capital in order to make systemic change. It's not that AWAKE doesn't seek systemic change, because it does. But when framed by the practices of emotional literacy, AWAKE's starting place is different. AWAKE has been and is still being shaped by hope. Jim Wallis, editor of *Sojourners* magazine, writes that "Hope means believing in spite of the evidence and then watching the evidence change."[2]

Turning Toward Wholeness

There are many signs that our congregation is turning toward multicultural wholeness. In addition to the AWAKE Ministries team initiating opportunities with UUCA's faith development programs (for children, youth, and adults), with emotional literacy at its foundation, it is helping to sustain prison, addictions, mentoring, and shelter ministries.

One of our most exciting programs is AWAKE's midweek worship service. It is emotive, embodied worship, with spirited music, coaching, praying, and witnessing; there's singing, laughing, shouting, dancing, and clapping.

Another sign of the congregation turning toward wholeness is that AWAKE is creating opportunities for some who think of themselves as Unitarian Universalist but have felt marginalized or

---

2   Jim Wallis, "A Prayer for Mandela," *Sojourners*, February 2014.

unwelcome in a traditional Unitarian Universalist setting. A mix of Unitarian Universalists attend the midweek worship: Unitarian Universalist seminarians and interns who seek to broaden their experience of liberal worship; Unitarian Universalists from area congregations; UUCA members who wish to strike a balance in their worship life; and Unitarian Universalist professionals who feel the absence of a worshipping community because they're working during traditional Sunday worship.

Sharing Unitarian Universalism is another way we are living the promises of Beloved Community. This is something we did not expect: AWAKE is becoming an interfaith ministry. Half of the midweek worship band belongs to other congregations. Becoming interfaith is a remarkable breakthrough, not just because of the theological differences that separate us but also because the wider community has historically been suspicious of UUCA, especially faith communities of color. (Their recent increased attendance and participation is the result of bridge-building by Rev. John Crestwell and our music director, Elizabeth Kraning, a retired public high school music teacher). We did not anticipate AWAKE midweek worship becoming interfaith, but as we look back, it now makes sense given the target audience and message, which was multiracial and theocentric leaning. We also hosted an interfaith Gospel Festival, created by the AWAKE Leadership Team, that filled the sanctuary. It was composed largely of singers and an audience from city congregations. Events like these create opportunities to dismantle traditional barriers that have divided communities of faith. Each of AWAKE's ministries is open to members and friends from other faith communities as well as the unchurched (the "nones"). Consequently, many are taking the Unitarian Universalist message back to their peers and congregations. In unique ways, these folks have become a part of our weekly life.

Another sign of our journey toward wholeness is a strengthening of Unitarian Universalism. When the UUCA reached four hundred members, we talked a lot about spinning off another congregation. District staff consulted with us, but in the end the idea was abandoned, even though planting a congregation is one of the traditional ways Unitarian Universalism has grown our association. But it has also met with overwhelming challenges: overhead costs, staff financing, and mixed loyalties of those from an existing congregation who are encouraged to attend the new congregation. While AWAKE Ministries could be described as a version of this traditional model, it has removed some of the obstacles. It is housed by and is a program of UUCA, which provides support and leadership from its members and ministry team. But AWAKE is about more than just adding another congregation to the Unitarian Universalist list of congregations. It is committed to a multicultural ministry in its outreach and worship—this is deliberate and intentional. It is strengthening our faith by deepening and broadening the experiences people have with church.

We Are Building a New Way

At AWAKE Ministries we are building a new way of being Unitarian Universalist. It is built on a framework that any congregation could adapt.

We engage in partnering. We do this in many ways: the AWAKE singers and band, the Gospel Festival, emotional literacy programming at the prison and the local shelter, our multigenerational Middle Hour and worship, and working with the UUA and other congregations. There are many opportunities, and we have done a good job of stepping up to those partnerships.

We have support. It comes from the UUA and UUCA members and friends. They have been generous and bold and shared their ideas and resources with us. We are thankful.

We have a leadership team charged with making the vision become a reality. In the congregation we serve, we have been blessed with a ministry team of three, a forward-thinking music director, and an annual intern.

We embrace that the learning never ends. We discovered that spending time outside our comfort zones is critical. We stepped back from assumptions about liturgy and music cadence, about the homeless and the incarcerated. We listened to the songs and prayers of those from another faith. We lived with the dis-ease of a worldview different from our own.

We have fun and share our feelings. Laughing and clapping, shouting and crying, hugging and dancing are part of worship and other ministries. This can be challenging for Unitarian Universalists, because we seem to be a religion of the left brain, but there's more to us than that. At AWAKE we bring our whole selves.

We are willing to commit. Clergy and other leaders had to commit to the congregation's vision. And more: we made a commitment to multicultural ministry and the people we serve, the kind of commitment that promotes honesty and boldness.

Finally, we are willing to go deep and to be vulnerable. Here's an example: We have monthly worship themes. Healing was the theme one month, and after a great deal of conversation, we decided to include in the Sunday worship a time for people to come forward and stand with a minister for personal prayer or healing. The ministry team had no expectation of what would happen with prayer or healing—we didn't know a person's expectations or motivation for coming forward, unless it was shared with us. We were surprised when people rose and came forward in small numbers at first, and then formed lines in front of each minister. We never polled participants afterward asking what they thought we meant or why they came forward, though the ministry team did have a conversation about the event. We remembered that a root origin of the word *religion* implies a binding together in order to make whole, as in to heal. It was in this spirit that participants came forward and the ministers responded. This practice continues at every AWAKE worship service. It's as though people were saying they wanted to go deep in prayer and reflection, in naming their pain or joy, to share what was on their heart, seeking encouragement or support. Many who remained seated told us how moving it was to see people come forward. Words of support and gratitude are also a regular part of midweek worship, where the desire to be moved and go deep is expected.

This is a different way of being and becoming Unitarian Universalist. While this is our congregation's story, we believe it is a journey any congregation can take to address the dawning future. Start the journey and create your own story.

Visit *www.awakeministries.us*
to learn more about this community

First Unitarian Church of Rochester, New York

The Unitarian Universalist Congregation of Canandaigua, New York

The Remedy of Connection: Theme-Based Church

KAAREN ANDERSON

Many years ago, at the two congregations I serve, First Unitarian Church of Rochester and The Unitarian Universalist Congregation of Canandaigua, New York, we started theme based church. Theme-based church is simple. Each month, one concept, theological precept, or way of being in the world unique to Unitarian Universalism sets the tone and content for that month's inquiry, engagement, and ministries. At the churches I serve, we use themes that directly speak to what it means to be a Unitarian Universalist by asking the question, What does it mean to be a person of . . . ? The themes might include Resilience, Evolution, or Letting Go, for instance. However, other theme-based churches use traditional church language, such as Prayer, Transformation, or God. It matters not. What matters is how much easier it is to offer comprehensive meaningful programming and services when you are not flitting around from one idea to the next.

We began with worship, music, and small group ministry. At first this new approach made me anxious. I worried that one of the other ministers might steal my angle for a sermon or that the worship theme might restrict my creative juices, boxing me in. I was also worried about our people. Might they get bored or feel so doused in a particular theme—grace or vulnerability or resilience—that they would be like groundhogs, not rearing their heads again until the first of the next month, when a new theme was introduced? Suffice it to say, I had reservations.

And yet, as life often does to me, I was surprised to find just the opposite. The congregation was elated with the change. They experienced the alterations as an opportunity to immerse themselves in worship rather than flitting from one topic to the next. They relished the chance to come at the theme from many different angles, and perhaps most important, the themes became their guide for their own musings, reflections, and reconnections to self, others, and the needs of the world. I benefitted professionally; I got to bounce ideas off my colleagues and inquire about their own musings or personal implications. The church's music director came with arrangements and choral pieces drawing on various aspects of the theme I never would have thought of myself. In the end, it made our work more collaborative not less.

In worship, the themes worked. But what hooked me was the corollary step of using the same themes in our small group ministry program. Ministers often say that we want parishioners to give of their time, talent, and treasure; we want them to understand that church is a co-op, not a consumer product or service. But this theme-based ministry work changed my perspective by changing the question from "What do we want *from* our people?" to "What do we want *for* them?" That's the better question to be asking. What I want for them is more compassion; to know their lives matter; to be spiritually connected to the grace of life, to their best selves, and to a larger community; to know that they, with others, can make a difference in the world. Only through theme-based ministry did this emphasis on what I wanted for them connect for me.

Perhaps one of the best ways to get at what I'm talking about is to explain the guts of what happens in a small group I lead. Each month we sit in a circle, do a check-in about our spirits, then dive into the spiritual assignment, reading, video, or question that captured our heart that particular month. We are a motley crew: two organic farmers, two environmental scientists, an MBA student, a special education teacher, an artist, a librarian, a retired CEO, a retired news anchor, a small-business goat-soap entrepreneur, and me. We are young and old, introverts and extroverts, patient and impatient, expressive and reserved, contemplative and impulsive. Yet with all our diversity, this little band of Unitarian Universalists manages to work with a monthly worship theme in depth. That's the magic of the small group work: the depth to which we can explore a particular theme.

I've been in the ministry almost twenty years. I've known the joy in worship when grace arises, and we are all connected, flawed, and fabulous together. I've sat with parishioners as they disclose their tales of woe: lies told, hopes dashed, revelation received. Over the years, I've loved these moments of ministry, yet none of them in their totality compare to the richness, the jaw-dropping courage and vulnerability that float through and around our little circle. When our Soul Matters group is together, there is no fixing, no saving, no setting each other straight. We offer each other space to hold one another's pain, elation, trepidation, anger, inspiration, tragedy, joy. It seems such a simple gift: Deep listening. Each person tells what assignment they completed, what story they sat with daily. Each one does this without interruption; no one is allowed to ask questions or offer a follow-up until we all have said our piece. My group is half men, half women. The men cry without embarrassment or worry that anyone will think less of them. The women rant, strutting their mighty testosterone with glee. We laugh; we weep. There has not been a month where stories aren't told about a spouse betrayal, family secrets that kept a person hostage, or the ongoing peeling back of layers of sadness associated with mental illness or addiction. But we also tell tales of the resurrection of one's spirit, the sharing and giving of unconditional love, the faith in our common, extraordinary, vibrant humanity that leans toward the light.

At the end of an evening, I often drive home in silence, running through what just transpired in the course of those two hours.

Every time, I am reminded how lucky I am that there are people who hold me, accept me, honor me, and encourage me. I come home each month with the best of who I want to be and become, and I have a net of forgiveness and trust to go back to when I've disappointed myself and others.

Our sessions together are not just an evening of good discussion or an opportunity for intellectual stimulation or even a chance to make new friends. Rather, they are a path back home. The Soul Matters groups are unlike other small group curricula that give people a time to reflect on the past. In our groups we explore how the theme, right now, spiritually connects us to greater mindfulness; to family, friends, co-workers; to our commitment to a life of service. The small groups are organic and central to everything we do now at both First Unitarian of Rochester and Unitarian Universalist Church of Canandaigua.

Small group ministry is so important that after new people go through the requisite steps toward membership, they are immediately placed into a Soul Matters group with their peers. These small groups become people's support networks, their lifelines in a harried world, and central to how they behave in and out of the group. In fact, they are so well embedded now in our church culture that oftentimes the group takes care of its members quicker and faster than any minister ever could. For instance, one parishioner tragically lost a child, and by the time the ministers got wind of it, her small group had claimed detail for food, laundry, and child care for her other child for months to come.

Worship, music, and Soul Matters were just the beginning of our theme-based church. Once the themes were firmly embedded in those ministries, we cast our net even farther. All our adult education and spiritual development groups came on board: from Buddhist discussion groups to guest speakers for social justice gatherings to our academic Bible study group taught by the local college's religious studies professor. Social justice task forces and ongoing ministry projects now had a means to further their mission when a particular theme resonated with their members and the church's monthly events. Most important, in my opinion, was the web of theme-based ministry integrated into religious education. Many parents have told us that they can now connect adult worship to their kids' worship and workshops to their small groups quite easily. Primarily because it offers a family a chance to see and talk about a theme, which has been explored from a four-year-old's perspective all the way through to a fifty-year-old's, and they can all talk about it as they pull out of the parking lot from church on their drive home.

Theme-based church is integral to how our church functions and behaves. I'm convinced the reason this works is because Unitarian Universalism is about connection. We are a religion that sees people struggling, not against our own sinful souls but against a shallow, frantic, and materialistic world that all too often leaves us disconnected. Our congregations—at their best—work to heal that divide by helping people listen to their deepest selves, open up to life's gifts, and serve needs greater than their own. In our congregation, Soul Matters, worship, religious education, and faith in action support this theology by embracing deep listening, which in turn sets the stage for us to welcome grace and the needs of the world.

As we do all this work, our theme-based ministry focuses us on a spiritual value that our faith tradition has historically honored and emphasized. We are reminded that our faith dreams of a preferred way for us to be in the world, challenging each of us to ask, What does it mean to live a life with these particular values front and center? Unitarian Universalism is not a religion of "anything goes." Rather, our faith has a unique vision of the good life. Yes, we affirm personal choice and individuality, but our faith asks us to engage some core values, take them seriously, and apply them to our daily living.

Both a theology of connection at our center and the particularity of the Unitarian Universalist life in practice are key to our growth at First Unitarian. In the last ten years, we've grown from a congregation of 700 members to 1,050. We've partnered with a small congregation (80 members) in Canandaigua, New York, for staff and resource sharing. But perhaps it's more accurate to say we've grown internally, which in the end is what matters. These people—the parishioners in these two congregations, in the Soul Matters group, in faith in action projects, in nonstructured, engaged conversation over coffee about the themes—make us better individually and as a community. They challenge, love, tweak, and kid me. They conspire against arrogance of thought and action. We remind each other to be patient with oneself and others. We're reminded that our inherent humor, wisdom, and courage are always available if we just make the effort to listen long enough. People do so because this theme-based church is integral to their living and loving. At times they lead me more than I lead them, often with a piercing insight and a vulnerability that opens the human condition to me with such courage and clarity that I feel weak in the knees. They often reflect that without this structure, without theme-based ministry, they'd feel a little bit like fish out of water. That's a powerful affirmation that the church is not only a place they go on Sunday or where they drop in for social justice activities but also the hub of where they find meaning, connection, and growth.

I believe this to be the center of the religious life in the twenty-first century. It is said that the twenty-first-century American feels they have, on average, one person to whom they can confide their fears, hopes, dreams, and worries. One? If one is the average, then that means a number of people are saying they have zero friends to confide in, to sort through what matters in life and what doesn't, zero connections to another's story for inspiration or solace, zero safety net when their life feels like they have to go it alone, zero depth in their living and loving. Zero. That's a scary number. Yet that zero makes theme-based ministry one of the best gifts we as Unitarian Universalists can offer. We've got the remedy for the sin-sick soul. We just need to apply it and live into our calling for the twenty-first century.

*Visit **www.rochesterunitarian.org** and **www.canandaiguauu.org**
to find out more about these communities*

Sacred Fire Unitarian Universalist, Carrboro, North Carolina

Circles of Community

NATHAN ALAN HOLLISTER

For the past two and a half years Sacred Fire Unitarian Universalist, based in Carrboro, North Carolina, has been bringing small group ministry out into the community, connecting with socially active, nonaffiliated Millennials. And it's working. We are forming relationships with those who aren't necessarily seeking church, but who share our values and our vision of the Beloved Community. We now have three chapters made up of multiple small group ministry "circles," in Carrboro, North Carolina; Brooklyn, New York; and Seattle, Washington. At the time of this writing, we plan to launch three more in 2015 and are raising the money needed to staff these expansions of our ministry. It's working that well.

The ministry of Sacred Fire is a growing movement within Unitarian Universalism, one that is relevant to our time and proving successful. While Sacred Fire's ministry is mostly with young adults who are new to Unitarian Universalism, the ministry is truly a deliberate partnership between Millennials and older generations of Unitarian Universalists.

Millions of seekers are out there. Hundreds of thousands of people identify as Unitarian Universalist and aren't involved in UU congregations. There are many, many more people who share our values and our vision of the Beloved Community. We have to come to grips with the reality that *most* of these seekers are not seeking church. Most of them are not going to become Unitarian Universalists, they are not going to come and worship on Sunday morning, they are not going to join our committees. But shared values and visions still bind us to one another. They are our people, and we are theirs. The only true difference is what forms of relationships we will build with one another. If not only congregations, then what?

Covenant as Through Line

Sacred Fire Unitarian Universalist exists to do two things: to increase our capacity for and effectiveness in social justice and to experiment with alternative forms of religious community that can form a future of our Unitarian Universalist faith. Our mission is to plant and grow covenanted communities with a spiritual praxis of social transformation.

The starting place is always relationship. Our UU faith informs us that all things are interconnected, and a prophetic vision is one that calls us to how we should be in relationship with one another and with that which is greater. For this we look to a theology of covenants. Covenants are the free, voluntary, mutual, and noncoercive promises that we make with each other and with that which is greater. As a noncreedal people, we know that we can't focus on finite and predetermined ends but rather to a prophetic vision. What we commit ourselves to, then, is a process of being human, to a specific quality of relationship.

Informed by this theology, a covenanted community can look like a great many things. The forms they take are not as important as the process they share. Existing Unitarian Universalist congregations are covenanted communities, to be sure, but there is the potential for myriad other expressions. It is some of these very expressions that our denomination is planting and growing. They can look like any number of things, and it is precisely this experimentation that our faith needs. In that experimentation, though, there needs be a through line that binds us together. We at Sacred

Fire understand that through line to be covenant, and the communities we create must be ones in which we expressly covenant with one another and with that which is greater. Covenant spells out commitment, it spells out a process through which we engage with one another and the world, it represents a deliberate attempt to be together.

At Sacred Fire, when we refer in our work to spiritual praxis, we mean it in a way quite distinct from spiritual practice. *Praxis* means to embody our spiritual and theological truths, to be transformed by that embodiment, and to reconstitute our truths in an ongoing process. We use this word out of a particularly stinging critique of what we UUs do. During the Spanish Revolution there was a popular saying that went like this: "Those who proclaim to have principles, but who have no programs [for social change], turn out in the end to have no principles." This is a monumental challenge for Unitarian Universalists if we simply capitalize the *P*. We have the Principles, but do we have a program for building the Beloved Community? How do we live out, in the here and now, our visions of interconnection, covenantal relationships, and the more beautiful world that our hearts know is possible?

A quote attributed to the early Unitarian Francis David maintains that "We need not think alike to love alike." This resonates powerfully still today. It is true that we need not think alike (and we probably shouldn't!). But I think the saying means more than that. It means that if we want to change the world we will have to learn to love alike. Our story is about learning to do that.

The Early Days: Meals and Thirsts

About six years ago a group of us started getting together regularly for potlucks. We chose Monday nights because, being mostly food service workers, that was the night most of us had off. From the outset Sunday mornings weren't really a possibility for us, as we either had worked until 3 a.m. on Saturday night or were working Sunday brunch. Monday nights became our time.

What began as a social gathering of friends and acquaintances evolved over time. Eventually we started asking, how can we ensure this doesn't stop? This question can be interpreted as a longing for formality or commitment to one another, at least at a baseline level. More than that, our discussions together deepened, and I was astounded to find the immense thirst for exploring questions of intimacy and ultimacy with one another. I was in divinity school at the time, so I would drift into these sorts of conversations with some regularity (ahem). The astounding thing was that here my friends were asking for more, were taking notes, were wanting to dig deeper. All the folks involved were not attached to any faith community, and as such they had few places to ask and discuss these sorts of questions.

Moving on from the concerns of how we would keep this thing going and how our thirst for meaning could be fulfilled, other, practical questions emerged, questions about how we could support each other in life. Being mostly low-income and under- or unemployed young people, this was an exceedingly important question. We were referring to making sure each of us could make rent, had good food to eat, had transportation or child care. This sort of thing is not typically answered in standard religious communities, but such questions have been answered by other traditions.

Looking to the black and immigrant churches we saw longstanding forms of mutual aid combined with religious community. A particularly inspiring example that we continue to draw from in our ministry is that of the Free African Society. This organization was created in the late 1700s by formerly enslaved people to fulfill their spiritual, social, and economic needs. In addition to holding religious services, the Free African Society also provided unemployment insurance, job skills training, health care, and more. When the Constitutional Convention was taking place in Philadelphia, a yellow fever epidemic broke out. While America's "founding fathers" fled the city to avoid contracting the illness, the Free African Society distributed food, medicine, and hundreds of blankets to the stricken populace.

These types of community support are rarely seen in Unitarian Universalist congregations. Moreover, UUs aren't possessed of the mindset that religious communities exist for such work. The class makeup of our congregations is such that many of us don't have to worry about having health care, making rent next month, or having a working vehicle. Therefore we don't set up mechanisms within our communities to address needs like these. When people come to Unitarian Universalist congregations seeking an expanded view of the needs we can serve, they don't find these mechanisms. These people are not likely to stay. And we perpetuate the lack of mechanisms for service by not recognizing widespread unmet needs. It becomes self-fulfilling.

For Sacred Fire, these roles are necessary, and in fact they became for us a spiritual practice. The questions that led us to co-create these mechanisms are simple: What are the barriers to community? What prevents us from spending time with one another, from deepening our bonds, from doing the things that make us whole? Here is where our work begins.

A number of the people who formed our nascent community were or had been actively involved in social justice work. In that work, many of us had forever encountered loneliness, isolation, frustration, and despair in the face of the injustice of the world and the attendant environmental devastation. Another question we began to ask was, how do we support each other in the pursuit of justice? For this work we have most strongly drawn on examples from the liberation theology movements in Latin America.

A powerful and challenging assertion of liberation theology—which emerged not only in Latin America but also among the black Protestant community in the United States during the late 1960s—is that if everything we claim about god, the universe, and life does not result in justice and mercy at this place in history, then it's not true. That is quite a litmus test for truth! It demands that our theologies, our ecclesiologies, and our practices in religious community result in real, incarnated justice. In Central and South America, poor and working class people organized themselves into base communities, which are deliberate communities of support for the task of incarnating justice. Just as we looked to the mutual aid traditions of the black church for ways to give each other life support, so we listened to the lessons from these base communities about how to live a faith geared toward the vision of the Beloved Community.

Our attempts to answer all these questions led us to organically evolve from informal potluck gatherings to a sustaining and justice-making community. That community is growing not only here in Carrboro where we started, but around the country.

Small Groups of Intimacy and Ultimacy

The primary vehicle for Sacred Fire's work is small group ministry. We regard small groups as the building blocks of humanness, and this is informed by a number of things. One is biology, which shows that humans are wholly dependent upon one another from the outset. The only response that can spring forth from this interdependence is gratitude. Another thing that informs us is anthropology, which shows the preeminence of the kinship group as the foundation of closely knit community. Third, working within the rubric of the small group helps us move in mindset and "heartset" away from the individualist notion "I think, therefore I am" to the relational pan-African philosophy of *ubuntu*. This philosophy says that I am because we are. Finally, in the pursuit of justice making, we take our cue from anthropologist Margaret Mead, who said, "Never doubt that a small group of thoughtful, committed people can change the world. Indeed it's the only thing that ever has."

Sacred Fire consists of communities made up of small groups that explore issues of intimacy and ultimacy. These groups form a support network for life, they deepen our faith, they strengthen our relationships with one another, they transform us, and they build community deliberately. Anyone wishing to participate in our communities joins a small group first, not the entire community. Participants then share in a group-learning curriculum that we have developed, called *Sacred Fire*. This eight-session (or single weekend) curriculum consists of action-reflection sessions on theology and philosophy, ethics and process, anti-oppression and community building, strategies of social transformation, and viable models of change. Once folks have completed these sessions, they become members of our communities.

This creates a higher bar for membership than most Unitarian Universalist congregations (although similar models are not uncommon in other denominations). The effect that it has, however, is quite interesting. I have always heard and been under the impression that the younger generation is not interested in membership or in pledging monetary support. We have found this to be false. Unitarian Universalists must collectively shift the way we think about membership and pledging. If membership consists of signing the book and promising to show up every once in a while, it doesn't hold much power for many people. It worked for me, but I grew up going to a UU congregation every Sunday; I had already been churched. But what about those who aren't churched, and don't want to be? For them, membership needs to hold meaning and power in a way they co-create. Our small group process builds that meaning and power. Regarding pledging, people give their resources to things to the extent that those things are relevant to their lives. That's it. If it's relevant, if it informs them, buoys them, supports them, helps them grow and realize their potential, produces results felt in the heart and in the hand and in the streets, then the resources flow in. Thus far, 100 percent of our members pledge.

Members of our chapters build community deliberately in three primary ways. First, as mentioned, are the monthly small group ministry sessions. Then, the larger community of multiple small groups and whomever else they invite gets together each month to *gather* and to *build*. These gatherings consist of a potluck meal, a ritual of togetherness, and a sharing of fellowship. After the meal, we discuss what is going on in our community and in the wider world, often focusing on our ongoing work and upcoming events.

Each month we also get together to build. This is a specific and immediately impactful project of some sort, much like an Amish barn raising. We might build community-share gardens, or construct a shed to use for a neighborhood tool share, or have a teach-in on canning food, or cook a meal for the annual meeting of a low-income resident-owned housing cooperative, or have an all-ages fun day, or build a ramp so that someone's home is more accessible. Whatever the project, it is easy for new people to come and participate. Younger folks in particular want something they can jump into and see the results of here and now. Talk alone bores us. We build to create shared experiences that both strengthen our community and raise our capacity for further action. What we are truly building is community, sometimes with a physically tangible project, every time tangible to the spirit.

In that deliberate community building, we have two centering practices that we collectively pursue: the spiritual practices (or praxes) of interdependence and solidarity. A praxis of interdependence works from the relational mindset to deepen our dependence on one another and our relationship with the planet upon which we live. A central praxis for our Carrboro chapter is co-creating a food justice system in our area. We cooperate to grow as much food as we can and coordinate to share it with one another. For what we can't grow ourselves, we form relationships with farmers and get the food directly from them. We have a system of purchasing groceries in bulk. We collect hundreds of pounds of donated local produce each week and distribute it to about fifty families in our area, most of whom recently immigrated and with whom we seek to be good neighbors. You might be asking yourself, this is religious community? Yes, it is. It is a community that embodies its prophetic vision.

During the era of the Social Gospel around the turn of the twentieth century, liberal religion shifted away from a focus on the individual to a focus on social salvation. Unitarian minister John Haynes Holmes wrote in his 1912 book *The Revolutionary Function of the Modern Church* that if our task is to redeem the social order, then all relationships become religious ones. He called upon us to make "religion . . . coincident with life." One way to describe this today is found in the UU hymn "Spirit of Life" by Carol McDade, when we sing that we are "giving life the shape of justice." Collective spiritual practice is growing and deepening our interdependence with one another, in this and many other ways.

Our spiritual praxis of solidarity focuses on ever-widening circles of community. When our congregations seek to become more multicultural, we usually focus on creating wonderful, welcoming spaces and inviting people to come into them. And the spaces we create are wonderful, and often they are welcoming too. But doing it only this way places 100 percent of the risk on others to come to us to see how cool we are. A missional mindset calls us to go to them, to meet people where they are, to operate in the community. Sacred Fire's strategy regarding growth, especially multicultural growth, is social justice work. And that work is about risk, for that's what solidarity requires.

An example of how we practice solidarity in our Carrboro chapter is our creation of Solidarity Network. This is a community organizing strategy that allows us to stand with our neighbors who are experiencing exploitation or discrimination in some way, usually in the realm of jobs or housing. So far, in our town, we have been active in solidarity with day laborers, who routinely experience wage theft (that is, they are not paid for agreed-upon work). We write letters in which the workers demand the pay they earned. Then we call all of our friends, and the workers call theirs, and we go with them to stand in silent witness as they deliver the letter. It works magnificently, especially when children and elders are present. It is a simple, direct, and effective method that usually creates immediate results (if the demand letter doesn't work, we get more creative). One of the greatest things about it, and one thing that makes it a spiritual practice, is that we surrender ourselves to the agenda of those directly experiencing the oppression. This too is what solidarity requires. Unitarian Universalists must prove that we are their people and that they are ours by standing alongside these others with whom we wish to be in relationship and in community.

A last piece to hold up about our methodology of social transformation is ensconced in a quote from Buckminster Fuller. He said that "You never change things by fighting the existing reality. To change something, build a new model that makes the existing model obsolete." This is how we work to change the world, by creating viable alternatives to unjust and environmentally unsustainable systems. This has its place strongly in Unitarian Universalist history. Our Congregationalist forebears practiced democracy in their religious communities for hundreds of years, making their own decisions and calling their own leaders. During the buildup toward the American Revolution, it was precisely these models that showed the way to a better nation. These congregations could be looked at as viable, working models of democratic community, and the question became, why doesn't all society look like this? Theodore Parker, John Haynes Holmes, and James Luther Adams have shared this narrative about our early congregations as inspiration for the American Revolution. What inspiring alternative models is your congregation practicing today? What inspiring models could Unitarian Universalists be practicing?

A "Go to Them" Approach

What Unitarian Universalism needs for its future—what it must do for its future—is to experiment with different forms and manifestations of its faith. We cannot rely solely on the old models, and we must also be actively taking risks to explore new forms. These new forms and methods must be accessible to those who do not see a home for themselves in our current models. Unitarian Universalist values resonate much farther than we presently see, and therefore Sacred Fire uses the missional or "go to them" approach in addition to the traditional attractional or "come to us" one. For in truth, what do we exist for? Why do we exist as Unitarian Universalists? Do we exist to build these particular institutions, our congregations and the Unitarian Universalist Association, or do we exist to build the Beloved Community? Our congregations and our UUA are vehicles for that pursuit, and they are vital, but they are not the reason for our existence.

Part of experimenting with new models means that we must focus on how we live our lives and not on what we call ourselves. Folks want a faith that is relevant to and embedded in their daily lives. Most people out there aren't going to identify *as* Unitarian Universalist, ever. But if we find ways to be in relationship with them, perhaps they'll identify *with* it. Perhaps they will if we show that we are partners in the process of building a better world of justice, wholeness, and sustainable ecology. The Abolitionist movement against slavery, Transcendentalism, and religious humanism all sprang—at least in part—from Unitarian and Universalist understandings, but they eschewed the label of their origins. Perhaps we can now have the broader vision that they did, and see that our particular names and form are transient. What is permanent is the content that we offer: authentic community, depth that is applicable to life, and compelling and effective methods for changing the world.

Do we have that courage? Should we begin our discussions with new people by telling them about Unitarian Universalism? Or should we begin by asking what they need, what makes them come alive, what we can teach one another? Should we begin by forcing ourselves to treat their allergic reaction to religious institutions or by talking about what we can build together?

At Sacred Fire we believe our purpose is to connect to and grow community with people who want to build the Beloved Community. And that's what we do. Some of our chapters don't identify as Unitarian Universalist, some do. We're more interested in how we are compelled to be and what we are compelled to do than with what we call ourselves. Our focus is to transform our relationships, and so our chosen labels become rather unimportant.

One group of folks who is immediately and powerfully attracted to what we're doing is my old friends from our youth program, Young Religious Unitarian Universalists (YRUU), who stopped going to church after they became adults. The proportion of young people who leave UU congregations hovers around 90 percent. My friends and I as youth in YRUU experienced a Unitarian Universalism that differed significantly from the type we encountered in the "adult congregations." Our worships were circular in style and often took place at night. Our communities were made up of small groups (Touch Groups) and our social justice work was much more radical than that of our parents (just as many Boomers can claim!). When I describe what we're doing here at Sacred Fire to these old friends, it's an easy sell, because it's closer to their experience of the faith. Many of these former YRUUers are the main organizers of our chapters.

Regarding financial sustainability, Sacred Fire's model is different here too. Many of our members have limited incomes. The pledging-units model alone won't suffice. Raising monetary support from the wider Unitarian Universalist community has been immensely difficult. Some of that, I believe, is my personal failing. Some of that, though, is our collective failing. This has been an excruciating part of our ministry. Our model is cheap, much, much cheaper than congregations. Once established, chapters fund themselves. Our work now consists of planting new chapters, coaching those who are growing them, and developing program materials and training for small group facilitators. Plus, there is administration and communication. For all of that, we need money.

A huge source of support for Sacred Fire early on was an extraordinarily generous Chalice Lighter grant from the Southeast District of the UUA. Without that and some smaller supporting monies from the district itself, we would not be here, at least not in this successful form. Last year we ran a successful campaign on Faithify, the UU crowd-funding website, and the generosity of the UU community allowed us to double our members. Later we received a similarly sized grant from the UU Funding Program, and we used it to double in size again. No congregations have stepped forward to directly support our work, but many in our area have graciously given us their collection plates on special Sundays. A growing number of individual Unitarian Universalists, however, see this vision as viable and have chosen to become Catalyzers, pledging money as outside supporters. Information on how to join that community is on our website.

We envision that will we become fully self-supporting in two main ways. First, our support strengthens with each new chapter. Our dream is to have a chapter in every single area cluster of congregations in the country. Together, with other congregations, we can become a truly transformative force in the world. The second way is something that might seem surprising to some. As we were casting about for alternative funding models—those that didn't rely on pledging units or outside grants and fundraising—we landed on one that has a 1,500-year run of success: monasteries. By the Rule of Saint Benedict, all monasteries must be self-supporting, so they do things like brew beer, run schools, farm, or raise livestock. Given that many of us are underemployed food service workers, it makes perfect sense for our communities to be incubators of craft industries that in turn support the communities themselves. At the time of this writing, we anticipate one of those outgrowths of our work, the Minister Book Exchange, in the fall of 2015.

Building the World We Dream About

So far Sacred Fire endeavors have been full of surprises. Those pieces that we thought would be quick took an interminable amount of time. Those pieces we regarded as complex and nigh insurmountable turned out to be simple. We've had to sink into the process and let it be. This is the way of co-creation. We don't— and can't—know exactly what our covenanted communities will become. Perhaps some of them will become congregations, but much more often they will become new expressions in the "beyond" of the Congregations and Beyond initiative.

Our faith calls on us to experiment with models of religious community that build the world we dream about. Sacred Fire is attracting (mostly, but by no means exclusively) young adult "nones" and the "dones," especially those who would fit into the category of what Martin Luther King Jr. called the "creatively maladjusted." They see and feel the injustice in our world, they yearn for authentic communities of support for their lives and for transformative possibility.

At Sacred Fire we're doing our best to build deliberate communities that practice interdependence and solidarity. We're doing it because we must. We're doing it because the faith needs us, and because the world needs us. We're doing it because there's no one else, and however we fumble along in our efforts, we can do nothing but try.

*Visit **www.sacredfireuu.org***
to find out more about this community

Postscript

A Letter to My Colleagues
and Those They Serve

Dear Colleagues and Friends,

Unitarian Universalism is at a turning point. All the indicators are there. In my sermons and conversations, I have named what looks clear to me: the transition and transformation of Unitarian Universalism from the errors of the iChurch to the promises of the Beloved Community—which is to say, the restorying of Unitarian Universalism from the trinity of errors to the trinity of promises. This will not result from wishful thinking, General Assembly resolutions, some Darwinesque natural institutional evolution, or even committed UUA leadership. As with many—maybe even most—changes to our way of faith, the transition and transformation must emerge with ministers and laity leading the way: The future of Unitarian Universalism is in our hands. Of course, laity will make this journey, but ministers especially must take the lead. Many will not want to fill this prophetic role.

In the opening pages of her book *The Power of Stories,* Jacqueline Lewis is clear and bold about leadership for the journey to Beloved Community:

I am convinced that this is a question of leadership. Leaders can, through their preaching, teaching, and developing other leaders, story a compelling vision in which cultural diversity is an ethical and moral imperative in the present, not a hope for the future. . . . I believe that each [of our congregations] is a *pocket of the promise* of the [Beloved Community]. . . . Even in the face of counter stories . . . congregational leaders can develop and sustain culturally diverse communities that reflect a vision of the peaceable realm.[1]

"We are the ones we've been waiting for," says the popular poem, but this is no mere gesture of goodwill or the wink of smugness. We are the ones who must begin building the bridge from errors to promises, from iChurch to Beloved Community. We all must be the leaders in this frame-bending process. The steps are clear, yet this ministry is challenging.

We must initiate the storytelling process. This is more than it appears, for it means we must become restorytellers who understand the telling and shaping of "the poetry of our roots," as folklorist Bill Ivey writes. Too often, I suspect, we are willing to affirm the stories members tell about Unitarian Universalism, unwilling to give a restoried explanation of who we could be. Perhaps it's just a simple thing, but, for example, I've quit repeating the shallow and often negative portrait of Unitarian Universalism painted by Garrison Keillor, John Updike, Kurt Vonnegut, and the many others who tell our story in a way that contemporary culture has absorbed and repeated so that it, for many, has become the normative narrative.

Our story will be told, let there be no mistake about that. But who gets to tell it? We must. We must choose to tell it in such a way that we acknowledge the trinity of errors but not make that the story. Our story is a future-directed one that draws on our trin-

---

1 Jacqueline J. Lewis, *The Power of Stories: A Guide for Leading Multi-Racial and Multi-Cultural Congregations* (Nashville: Abingdon Press, 2008), 1–2.

ity of promises, promises that restory Unitarian Universalism into tomorrow.

Gerald Hiestand, an evangelical Christian scholar and parish minister, convincingly makes a case for pastor-theologians of the sort of which I believe Unitarian Universalism is in short supply. He writes, "Theologians, in the main, no longer reside in the parish. The pastor-theologian has been replaced by the professor-theologian." The professor-theologian is a new development. For centuries, all theology was instigated and often developed in the congregation, from the pulpit. Hiestand argues for a reemergence and reimagining of ecclesial theology, which is "anything relevant to the mission and life of the church. And it addresses these issues not merely as an academic exercise—a raw quest for knowledge —but with the conscious and preeminent aim of building the church," that is, the Beloved Community. He concludes, "We won't change the world by reforming the academy. But we will . . . change the world by renewing the church."[2]

Ecclesiology, the way our congregations are structured and work, is shaped by good storytelling built on a theology rooted in the trinity of promises. Our role as professional and congregational leaders is to give the people we serve a Unitarian Universalist narrative that is worth repeating, a story that is accurate and a story that speaks to the future we choose to be; this story is not to be found not among the trinity of errors. That is a counterstory, a dead end.

Friends and colleagues, we are embarking on subversive ministry and leadership over and against a theology and ecclesiology four centuries in the making. Church members and ministers, it is imperative that you restory your congregation's narrative and share it with those yearning to breathe the vitality of Unitarian Universalism. Be prepared to lead, you must want to lead; we must anticipate resistance from those we serve and even from some col-

2 Gerald Hiestand, "Ecclesial Theology and Academic Theology: Why We Need More of the Former," *Reformation 21*, Alliance of Confessing Evangelicals, August 2009, www.reformation21.org/articles.

leagues and community members. This call will require us to make the following commitments:

A first commitment is to share the trinity of promises, its vision for Unitarian Universalism and how it can be lived in the congregation you serve or attend. Transparency is important— let there be no hidden agendas and let there be no apologies. The message "change or die" has been said by many, in different ways, and is one we too must hear. Tell the story of "the poetry of our roots," tell the story of who we are becoming.

Another commitment is to educate your congregation, educate yourself, create a network of trusted allies who support restorying. Spread the word from the pulpit and newsletters, urge your board and other congregational leaders to make this restorying their work too. Look to see how the promises are embraced and articulated in your congregation's faith development program.

A final and maybe the most important commitment is to learn how to lead this dramatic shift. Seek or use the authority of your ministry and leadership to imagine your congregation's future. If you don't feel you have this authority, consider why you don't. Often it's a matter of creating a tipping point, building to that place where change has a life of its own. Interview others who can help create enthusiasm and structure for this change, and find a way to bring them to your people, which could help you earn the trust needed to imagine and restory for change.

This leadership will also have a pastoral aspect. As we hear and read about demographic shifts, as we watch the "browning of America," we recognize that our ethnic-like faith will become increasingly isolated, and we have every reason to believe there will be ever-increasing tensions in our congregations—relationships will be strained. Generosity, pluralism, and imagination require us to stretch and deepen, and it will be necessary for the spiritual and pastoral leaders in our communities to hold the anxiety that inevitably will result from such change. Jacqueline Lewis says that how leaders hold stories facilitates the steady progress of development. She concludes: "The quality of the holding environment is about the behavior of those who hold."[3] Which is to say, leaders must model how the people they serve will embrace leaving the iChurch and shaping the Beloved Community.

This pastoral ministry will be both challenging and rewarding because of the deep and tender as well as hurt and angry feelings that will well up. Leaders may need to walk with those who are reluctant, who can't keep their eyes on the prize—who may not see the prize—whose experience and fear tells them to abandon the community (and its leaders). Yes, walk with them, but don't stop moving toward that tipping point. There will be those who want to bring it all to a halt. Getting started again could take an effort beyond a congregation's ability. For an example we have only to look at the Unitarian Universalist Association. How often has the UUA appeared to be moving ahead only to slowly come to a crawl, while those still on board the train called Promise wonder when we'll get going again?

Some will wonder what's spiritual about any of this. Living a life grounded in a posture of generosity, in a diverse community where people don't just tolerate but engage each other, living with an imagination that pushes us outside the orthodox, constrained ways of a reluctant if not fear-driven secular culture: This is the trinity of promises, this is Unitarian Universalism. It is a spiritual and spirited way of faith.

So ingrained are the trinity of errors in our way of faith that I know many Unitarian Universalists will not accept and hold the trinity of promises as a practice. I saw this reflected in two gatherings. One was a meeting with the ministers, members, and friends at the congregation I serve. I structured the conversation using appreciative inquiry (AI), explained the process to the forty people in attendance, and then went about discussing church programs. Most understood the value of AI and found the shift of approach refreshing. But several, at the end of the night, wondered when it would be time to problem-solve, to deconstruct the issues that were bothering them. This highlights the left-brained,

---

3 Lewis, 45.

critique-and-criticize approach that often exists during Sunday
morning worship. Is it little wonder that many visitors experience
Unitarian Universalism as religious but not spiritual? Let's face it:
Unitarian Universalists are reluctant to embody worship in all the
ways that it could be done (and still be a liberal faith)—that is, to
be present to worship with one's whole body and spirit.

Unitarian Universalists also must grow accustomed to testify-
ing. UUs are actually quite good at bearing witness to their faith,
which is simply telling one's personal religious and spiritual story.
You have likely attended or led a newcomers class and have experienced when people started telling their faith journey and you can't
turn them off! It's really quite remarkable for a people who sound
so reluctant to share their faith. Just before summer, I was explaining to a group that during their summer travels it was likely that
religion and church would come up in their conversations with
other travelers. "When you share that you are Unitarian Universalist," I suggested to them, "be prepared to get the proverbial stare,
then silence, and then a 'What's that?'" I urged them not to launch
into explaining the history or listing the Principles. These can be
found on the Internet. You see, I'm convinced that when people
ask about Unitarian Universalism, what they really want to know
is your story—of how and why you are a UU. Storytelling is vital
and viral.

Diana Butler Bass, a leading commentator on religion and
church in the United States, writes:

> All congregations, and all churchgoers, have faith stories.
> But for much of the twentieth century, mainline Protes-
> tants believed that it was somehow impolite or rude to
> talk about religion. Faith was deeply privatized, an inter-
> nal matter between the baptized and God. Devotional
> practices were also private. Indeed, people thought that
> to talk about faith somehow cheapened it. In that era,
> Protestants were taught that it was better to walk than
> talk, taking James's injunction that "faith without works
> is dead" far more seriously than most Christians through-

out history. Social justice, charity, caring for the poor, organizing soup kitchens—mainline Protestants did good works to demonstrate their devotion. Reverence for God meant silence and service. Churchgoers, like those [in our congregations], experienced the power of faith in the world through that service. But for many, there was no faith vocabulary, no way of talking about the God whom they served. With no words, it became surprisingly easy to forget the stories. Perhaps this is why both the ancient Hebrews and early Christians wrote down their experiences of God. Without the words, faith would be lost, the service rendered secular. By the end of the twentieth century, mainline Protestantism appeared, to many observers, as faith-less—a silent religion with no story to tell. Would a contemporary James change his mind? For the last few decades, mainline Protestantism seems to prove the case: faith without words is dead.[4]

For decades now, common wisdom has said that to change the world, to change our congregations, to transform communities and lives we have to walk our talk. Yet, here is Diana Butler Bass, one of the nation's premier liberal church historians, wondering whether we have been walking so much we've forgotten how to talk about it, that maybe we need to restory ourselves and learn the words (again).

A tsunami of culture change is about to overwhelm us while so many congregations and their leaders go about rehearsing drills for a spring shower. After the plain has been flooded, people's first response will be to pick up the pieces and go about constructing life as it once was. But there will be no going back, not if we are to shape a vital and vibrant congregational life that speaks of the future—the errors of our past will not work as the promises of tomorrow.

---

4 Diana Butler Bass, Foreword to Lillian Daniels, *Tell It Like It Is: Reclaiming the Practice of Testimony* (Lanham, MD: Rowman & Littlefield, 2005), x–xi.

Three decades have passed since Unitarian Universalist historian Conrad Wright offered this conclusion, one that sounds like it could have been spoken at a recent General Assembly:

> So the fate of religious liberalism rests with us. We may cling to the old paradigm, proclaim individual freedom of belief as an absolute value, and neglect of corporate worship as our inalienable right. Then we may dwindle in numbers and influence until we end up a museum piece, like the Shakers, the Schwenkfelders, and the Swedenborgians. But on the other hand, we may learn how to relate to new social forces, to master a new paradigm. If so, we may not simply assure our own survival as a segment of the Church Universal, but we may even contribute something to the humanizing of what threatens to be a far less comfortable world than the one you and I have known.[5]

Take great care, friends and colleagues. The dawning future waits. Yes, the path is challenging, it will often feel like the wind is not at our backs but blowing straight and hard on us. So let us remember, this is a journey not to be taken alone, which is why I write to you. Let us take this journey together. We can dance and sing, laugh and cry, and work hard to restory, reimagine, and rehearse "the poetry of our roots." The promises of tomorrow are so bright.

—Fredric Muir

---

5 Conrad Wright, "Walking Together: Individualism in Historical Perspective," in *Walking Together: Polity and Participation in Unitarian Universalist Churches* (Boston: Skinner House Books, 1989), 166.

Further Reading

Wayne Arnason and Kathleen Rolenz, *Worship That Works: Theory and Practice for Unitarian Universalists*. Boston: Skinner House, 2008. A practical guidebook for revitalizing worship life, with insights gleaned from an 18-month road trip in search of innovation in worship.

Assembled 2012: Select Sermons and Lectures from the General Assembly of the Unitarian Universalist Association. Boston: Skinner House, 2012. The major presentations of the Social Justice General Assembly in Phoenix, Arizona.

Thom Belote, ed. *The Growing Church: Keys to Congregational Vitality.* Boston: Skinner House, 2010. An invitation to experience the progress of several vital, expanding Unitarian Universalist congregations.

Marjorie Bowens-Wheatley and Nancy Palmer Jones, *Soul Works: Antiracist Theologies in Dialogue*. Boston: Skinner House, 2002. Bold truth-telling about the complex and pressing issues of racism in theology.

John Buehrens and Rebecca Parker, *A House for Hope: The Promise of Progressive Religion in the Twenty-First Century*. Boston: Beacon

Press, 2011. A call for liberals to claim the transforming power of their theological heritage as they undertake to advance social change.

Burton Carley and Laurel Hallman, eds. *Not for Ourselves Alone: Theological Essays on Relationship.* Boston: Skinner House, 2014. Personal stories and thoughtful reflections from Unitarian Universalist leaders on moving from individual identity toward relational connectedness.

Commission on Appraisal, *Who's in Charge Here?: The Complex Relationship Between Ministry and Authority.* Boston: Unitarian Universalist Association, 2013. The historical and social context behind Unitarian Universalists' struggles with authority and ministry, and how the conflicts can be addressed.

Robert Hill, *The Complete Guide to Small Group Ministry: Saving the World Ten at a Time.* Boston: Skinner House, 2003. A classic text on creating and sustaining covenant groups.

Leslie Takahashi Morris, James (Chip) Roush, and Leon Spencer, The *Arc of the Universe Is Long: Unitarian Universalists, Antiracism, and the Journey from Calgary.* Boston: Skinner House, 2009. Chronicles the recent history of the UUA in its struggles to become a more inclusive, multicultural movement.

Mark Morrison-Reed, *Darkening the Doorways: Black Trailblazers and Missed Opportunities in Unitarian Universalism.* Boston: Skinner House, 2011. An open-eyed look at the personal struggles and triumphs of African-American Unitarian Universalists.

Jean Nieuwejaar, *Fluent in Faith: A Unitarian Universalist Embrace of Religious Language.* Boston: Skinner House, 2012. A vision of how Unitarian Universalists can both deeply feel and deeply express their faith. Continues the conversation about a "Language of Reverence" sparked by Rev. William Sinkford.

Paul Rasor, *Reclaiming Prophetic Witness: Liberal Religion in the Public Square*. Boston: Skinner House, 2012. An inspirational call for religious liberals to bring their religious convictions to bear on the issues of our time.

Gil Rendle and Alice Mann, *Living Into the New World: How Culture Affects Your Congregation*. Herndon, VA: Alban Institute, 2003. How the drift from deferred pleasure to instant gratification, the increasing emphasis on the individual, and a shift from a culture of sameness to one of diversity have changed the mission of faith communities.

Christine Robinson and Alicia Hawkins, *The Deep Connections Series*. Boston: Skinner House.

Heart to Heart: Fourteen Gatherings for Reflection and Sharing (2009)

Soul to Soul: Fourteen Gatherings for Reflection and Sharing (2011)

Listening Hearts: Fourteen Gatherings for Reflection and Sharing (2015)

Innovative small group ministry sessions based on sharing and listening rather than back-and-forth discussion.

About the Contributors

Kaaren Anderson is the senior minister at First Unitarian Church of Rochester, New York, and the lead minister at the Unitarian Universalist Church of Canandaigua, New York. The Planned Parenthood Federation of America's Clergy Advisory Board presented her with the Distinguished Clergy Service Award in 2011 for launching the post-abortion talkline Connect and Breathe. She and her husband have three children.

Heather Concannon serves as the assistant minister of youth and families at the Unitarian Universalist Church at First Parish in Sherborn, Massachusetts. A lifelong Unitarian Universalist, she has been involved in youth and young adult ministry, campus ministry, and youth camps at Rowe Camp and Conference Center. She is a founding and current board member of Unitarian Universalist Community Cooperatives, the parent organization of the Lucy Stone Cooperative, where she has lived since 2011.

Terasa G. Cooley is the program and strategy officer for the Unitarian Universalist Association. She has also served as director of congregational life at the UUA and as district executive of the Mass Bay District. Prior to joining UUA staff, she served as parish minister in Hartford and Stratford, Connecticut, as well as in Chicago and Detroit.

John T. Crestwell Jr. is the associate minister of outreach, leadership, and evangelism at the Unitarian Universalist Church of Annapolis, Maryland, where he also leads AWAKE Ministries. He serves on the UUA President's Council, on the boards for Hospice of the Chesapeake and the National Institutes of Health, and is a member of the affiliate faculty at Meadville Lombard Theological School. He is married with a blended family of five children, ages 12 to 22.

Nathan Alan Hollister is the lead minister of Sacred Fire Unitarian Universalist. He is the grandson of a couple that helped to organize four Unitarian Universalist congregations. He was active in the national leadership of Young Religious Unitarian Universalists and has been a community organizer since he was a teenager. He lives and makes trouble with his partner Maddie in Carrboro, North Carolina.

Tamara Lebak is a Unitarian Universalist minister, published author, Gestalt-trained organizational development consultant and internationally certified executive coach. She is focused on increasing social and emotional intelligence and cultural competency, enhancing authentic expression, and ultimately creating a more just and compassionate world. She is a lover of pit bulls, a singer-songwriter, and proud mother of one.

Jacqueline J. Lewis is senior minister at Middle Collegiate Church in New York City and executive director of The Middle Project. She is a nationally recognized author, speaker, and preacher on the topics of racial, economic, and gender/LGBTI justice. She has been featured on NPR's Weekend Edition, CNN, *Essence* magazine, the Associated Press, and *The New York Times*. She is married to her best friend, John Janka, with whom she works for racial reconciliation every day.

Ian White Maher was raised Unitarian Universalist at South Church in Portsmouth, New Hampshire, and remained active as a teen and young adult. He worked at the Unitarian Universalist Association for two years in the Faith in Action Department. He served the Unitarian Universalist Congregation of Queens, New York, for six years before starting Original Blessing in Brooklyn. He is taking the year off to live in India and work on a book.

Rebekah A. Montgomery is a licensed professional counselor and the assistant minister at the Unitarian Universalist Congregation of Rockville, Maryland. She is also a reserve component military chaplain and was deployed to Afghanistan for an eighteen-month tour of duty. She was named "Military Chaplain of the Year" and received a Distinguished Service award from the Military Chaplains Association. She lives in Bethesda with her two children.

Peter Morales is the president of the Unitarian Universalist Association, following his election in 2009. Previously, he served as the senior minister at Jefferson Unitarian Church in Golden, Colorado. He has also served as the director for district services at UUA, and sat on the UUA Board of Trustees, the Mountain Desert District board, and on the Executive Committee of the Unitarian Universalist Ministers Association.

Fredric Muir serves as the senior minister of the Unitarian Universalist Church of Annapolis, Maryland. He is a board member of the Unitarian Universalist Legislative Ministry of Maryland and the UUA ambassador to the Unitarian Universalist congregations of the Philippines. He has also served on the executive committee of Unitarian Universalist Ministers Association, where he held the portfolio of Good Offices.

Parisa Parsa is a minister who has served within and beyond congregations since 1998. She has served with the Unitarian Universalist Urban Ministry, the Faithful Fools Street Ministry, and First Parish in Milton, Massachusetts. She is currently the executive director of the Public Conversations Project. She lives in Arlington, Massachusetts, with her family.

Erik Martínez Resly is a minister who founded and now leads The Sanctuaries, a racially and religiously diverse arts community in Washington, DC. It promotes spiritual growth and social change through the creative arts. He also enjoys screen printing, photography, and breaking it down on the dance floor.

 **David Ruffin** spent years working as a professional actor in New York City. Later, as a seminarian, he brought together a team of fellow students and musicians to found The Sanctuary Boston. After two years coordinating Sanctuary, he came to All Souls Unitarian Church in Tulsa, Oklahoma, to serve as their resident minister.

 **Thomas Schade** is a retired minister living in Ann Arbor, Michigan. From 1999 until 2013, he served the First Unitarian Church (Second Parish) in Worcester, Massachusetts, in various capacities, ending as the senior minister. He also served in the leadership of the UU Christian Fellowship, where he was president, 2003–2004. He has two adult daughters, three grandchildren, and two little dogs.

 **Carlton Elliott Smith** joined the Southern Region Congregational Life Staff of the UUA in August 2013. He lived for five months in France as a student guest-worker after college, and five months in Switzerland as a student at the World Council of Churches Ecumenical Institute following graduate school. As a Henry Luce Foundation Fellow, he wrote full-time for Religion News Service. He lives in his hometown of Holly Springs, Mississippi.

 **Mark Stringer** began serving as minister to the First Unitarian Church of Des Moines, Iowa, in 2001. He serves as the board chair for Project IOWA, a workforce development effort aimed at training workers to move from low-wage jobs to career-track employment. He lives in Des Moines with his wife, Susan, and their two daughters.

Christina Leone Tracy is the faith development minister at the Unitarian Universalist Church of Annapolis and has served in that role since 2011. She is a graduate of Meadville Lombard School of Theology and lives in Hyattsville, Maryland, with her husband Brian and their two dogs.

Rowan Van Ness is a founder and member of Unitarian Universalist Community Cooperatives and currently resides at the Lucy Stone Cooperative in Boston, Massachusetts. She has been transformed by living in community. She serves as a director of lifespan religious education at a local Unitarian Universalist congregation and enjoys hiking and creating pottery in her free time.

Cheryl M. Walker has served as minister to the Unitarian Universalist Fellowship of Wilmington since 2009. Prior to that, she served four years as the assistant minister at the Unitarian Church of All Souls in New York City. She has served on several national committees for both the Unitarian Universalist Ministers Association and the Unitarian Universalist Association. She currently resides in Wilmington, North Carolina, with her partner Elizabeth.

Kimberly Wildszewski serves as minister to the Unitarian Universalist Church at Washington Crossing in Titusville, New Jersey. She is a lifelong Unitarian Universalist and is proud to have served as ministerial intern at the Unitarian Universalist Church of Annapolis. She and her wife Tara live in Lambertville, New Jersey.